Divorce and Loss

Divorce and Loss

Helping Adults and Children Mourn When a Marriage Comes Apart

Joshua Ehrlich

ROWMAN & LITTLEFIELD
Lanham • Boulder • New York • London

Published by Rowman & Littlefield
A wholly owned subsidiary of The Rowman & Littlefield Publishing Group, Inc.
4501 Forbes Boulevard, Suite 200, Lanham, Maryland 20706
www.rowman.com

16 Carlisle Street, London W1D 3BT, United Kingdom

British Library Cataloguing in Publication Information Available

Library of Congress Cataloging-in-Publication Data

Ehrlich, Joshua.
Divorce and loss : helping adults and children mourn when a marriage comes apart / Joshua Ehrlich.
pages cm
Includes bibliographical references and index.
ISBN 978-1-4422-3181-8 (cloth : alk. paper) -- ISBN 978-1-4422-3182-5 (electronic)
1. Divorce--Psychological aspects. 2. Loss (Psychology) 3. Families--Psychology. 4. Family psycho-therapy. I. Title.
HQ814.E39 2014
306.89--dc23
2014005981

Printed in the United States of America

Contents

Acknowledgments

I am grateful to my many friends and colleagues who supported this venture. I specifically would like to thank my dear friend Hernan Drobny for his feedback, especially his pushing me to make the writing more user-friendly. I also am grateful to Michael Singer and Mary Whiteside, experts in children, families, and divorce, whose generous and incisive feedback provided both guidance and reassurance. Mary Brady, Rebecca Sestili, and Salman Akhtar each played an important supportive role in the early stages of this project.

This is a book in significant part about loss, and I want to acknowledge three people in my life whom I lost too early. Neil Kalter, my mentor in divorce-related work, blended tough-mindedness and tenderness in a way that continues to serve as a model. Joshua Newberg, my college friend, remains a presence in my mind. My mother's commitment to writing—as a poet, an editor, and reader—serves as an inspiration. I do not think it is a coincidence that two of my sisters and I were writing books at the same time.

I am grateful to Amy King and Rowman & Littlefield for their confidence in this project. Elyssa Shea provided helpful research assistance. Cindy Hyden toiled for many hours with me in revising and refining this book. I appreciate her attention to the nuances of language as well as the book's "architecture."

My son-in-law, Dirk Scheidt, has been a steady and loving presence throughout the writing of this book, as have my father and three sisters. My beloved children, Anna and Alexi, pressed me for years to write. I am deeply grateful to them for their encouragement and their love. Above all, I am grateful to my wife, Lena, for her steadfast love, her wisdom, and her support during even the most trying moments. None of this would have been possible without her.

Introduction

In my clinical work over twenty-five years with hundreds of divorcing and post-divorce families, I have found that family members must embark on mourning processes in response to the many losses of divorce if they are going to move on with their lives. Understanding individuals' disturbing feelings about separation and loss—and their defenses against these feelings—is a key step to understanding the dilemmas our patients bring to our offices, be they depressed adults unable to come to terms with a divorce, enraged adults spoiling for a fight, children who are heartbroken that their parents have divorced, or parents who can no longer connect with them. Johnston and Campbell (1988) observe that the literature on divorce is permeated by descriptions of the "loss and the recovery process as one akin to mourning" (p. 102). I am suggesting here that the loss and recovery process following divorce is not "akin" to mourning, but represents an actual mourning process. While many authors cite the role of mourning in divorce, none provide a detailed explication of the mourning process or give it the stature that I do in framing the psychological reactions to divorce and its importance in determining interventions.

After a divorce, some people are able to reconstitute their lives and move on. Others never recover. How can we understand that phenomenon? I will do so by examining the defenses people employ to manage the painful feelings and internal conflicts stimulated by separation and loss, and by addressing how these defenses either allow for constructive mourning or obstruct it. We will see that it is people's capacity to bear sorrow, hurt, and guilt that allows them to move forward and re-engage with relationships and other ventures. In the absence of that capacity, people are unable to mourn and can become paralyzed emotionally.

In a clinical setting, one often sees adults who remain hurt and furious years after a marriage has ended. Clearly, constructive mourning stalled for them. The concept of failed mourning provides a framework for understanding many of the negative outcomes of divorce for adults, including the protracted conflict one sees in the *high-conflict* divorce.

One of the great tragedies of divorce is that parents absorbed in their own mourning cannot easily tune in to their children's emotional reactions to loss. I suggest that the intersection between parents' mourning and children's mourning is where communication tends to break down, contributing to children's sense of loneliness and isolation in the post-divorce family. Throughout the book, I will emphasize how therapists can function as facilitators of mourning and also how they can help parents facilitate mourning for their children.

Divorce confronts clinicians themselves with emotional challenges. At its core, divorce involves wrenching separation and loss, at least at the outset. It is disturbing and frightening for all of us to see love relationships fail, especially when those relationships turn bitter. The devastation that accompanies the disintegration of a marriage evokes clinicians' own experiences of loss, and serves as a stark reminder that even the best-laid plans for a shared life of closeness and joy can fall apart. Furthermore, it is jarring for clinicians to see parents manifesting gross lapses in empathy that so obviously harm their children. And it is enormously dismaying when divorcing parents become so entangled with each other that they cannot move on with their lives.

In order to be fully engaged with our patients' sorrow around divorce—grownups and children alike—we as clinicians must learn to be aware of, and develop the capacity to tolerate, the sadness their sadness evokes in us. If we cannot bear their sorrow, we are prone to withdraw by, for example, becoming impatient or emotionally distant. We also are vulnerable to aligning with their defensive needs to fend off painful affects by buying into one adult's anger at the other, and in that way contributing to escalation of feuds between ex-spouses and interfering with productive therapy.

Optimally, working with divorce offers clinicians the chance to re-engage their own experiences of loss usefully, using painful feelings evoked by the clinical work to catalyze self-understanding. Those therapists working with high-conflict divorces must be prepared to deal with intense affects, especially rage. Therapists who fail to handle the challenges of high-conflict divorces constructively are bound to get into clinical and ethical difficulties.

As a practicing psychoanalyst who also does divorce work that spans the spectrum from mediation, custody evaluation, and parenting coordination to therapy with children, adolescents, and adults, I straddle two worlds. Those worlds converge in this book.

In every clinical contact, I view people through a psychoanalytic lens. I attune myself to their defenses against intolerable feelings and unwelcome impulses and, in working with adolescents and adults, assume that their difficulties in the present have antecedents in their childhood pasts. In seeking to understand my interactions with my patients, I attend carefully to transference and countertransference experiences, examining the meanings of my patients' fantasies and feelings about me and mine about them. In working with families in the throes of divorce, I attune myself to the interpersonal issues that are the bread and butter of family therapists. I try to understand environmental factors that stress children and adolescents and find ways to reduce them; I also try to pinpoint interpersonal factors that entangle and otherwise absorb divorcing spouses.

Psychoanalysis offers a rich framework for understanding the depth of human experiences, including divorce. Unfortunately, psychoanalytic ideas, complex and rapidly evolving, are seldom integrated into clinical thinking and research on divorce. It is my conviction that we need those ideas in order to address the complexity of the divorce experience. Otherwise, essential information is lost. As one brief example, I think about what might appear to be an obvious idea from a research paper on forgiveness following divorce: "It is not surprising that divorce often engenders long-lasting negative feelings because it can adversely impact many aspects of one's life" (Rye et al., 2004, p. 32). The authors cite such negative effects as social isolation, lower standard of living, and increased challenges raising children. As a psychoanalyst, I would argue that divorce engenders long-lasting negative feelings not only because of such relatively concrete consequences but also because of what it *means* psychologically to divorcing individuals.

The need for cross-fertilization cuts both ways. Many psychoanalysts have no more exposure to mainstream (i.e., non-psychoanalytic) writing on divorce than mainstream clinicians have to psychoanalytic ideas. As one important example, I would guess that few psychoanalysts know Jan Johnston's seminal work on the high-conflict divorce, even though they provide therapy or psychoanalysis to individuals mired in protracted litigation and acrimony. Yet clinicians dealing with high-conflict divorces need to understand the terrain they are wandering into or they can easily get lost—with potentially dire results.

While some psychoanalysts have approached divorce from a psychoanalytic perspective (e.g., Gunsberg and Hymowitz, 2005), some prominent mainstream clinicians have integrated psychoanalytic ideas and systems theory in their writings on divorce. Jan Johnston (1988, 2009), one of the foremost writers and researchers on divorce, offers a compelling, textured analysis of the high-conflict divorce that incorporates three interlocking perspectives: psychodynamic, interpersonal, and social systems. Judith Wallerstein (1980, 1989, 2000), the best-known writer on divorce, incorporates psychodynamic ideas into her clinical formulations, enriching them immensely. Neil

Kalter (1990), a brilliant divorce clinician and researcher, integrated psychodynamic ideas seamlessly into his clinical formulations.

In this book, I approach divorce through a psychoanalytic lens on mourning that focuses on people's ability to tolerate and come to terms with the painful emotions catalyzed by the coming apart of a marriage. While the concept of mourning is usually applied to loss by death, psychoanalysts—starting with Freud in 1917—have thought about mourning as the psychological response to various losses, including the relinquishing of certain core fantasies and the losses that inhere in the process of growing up.

This book divides into two parts. In part I, I address the impact of divorce on children, adolescents, and adults. Because one cannot understand the experience of divorce without understanding marriage, I begin by exploring in chapter 1 psychological functions of marriage and the multiple losses that ensue when it comes apart. I examine spouses' psychological reactions to these losses, including defensive efforts to cope with deep pain. Chapter 2 discusses mourning—what constructive mourning looks like, how challenging it is even in the best of circumstances, and how, when it goes well, a person grows.

People unable to tolerate the feelings necessary to mourn become mired in feelings of bitterness and inadequacy. Chapter 3 addresses failures of mourning, drawing on Vaillant's (1977) constructs of *immature* and *psychotic* defenses. It examines the high-conflict divorce as an exemplar of failed mourning and looks closely at the dynamics that crystallize the essential features of all divorce. Chapters 4 through 6 consider how the emotional challenges of parents as they work to extricate themselves emotionally from marriage affect their ability to attend to their children. They explore the convergence between parents' mourning and children's struggles to deal with the coming apart of their families.

Part II, building on the framework established in part I, introduces interventions. Chapter 7 looks at how facilitating person (e.g., parent, therapist) can help a child or adult mourn. Chapters 8 and 9 concentrate on interventions with parents, offering specific recommendations as to how clinicians can help parents counteract the potentially harmful effects of divorce on children. It addresses, for example, how parents can reduce conflict and improve parenting arrangements, as well as helping parents build meaningful connections with their children. Chapter 10 assesses the powerful pushes and pulls that high-conflict divorces exert on clinicians and offers suggestions for how to manage the pressures to avoid pitfalls and intervene productively.

Chapter 11 examines how therapists can help children and adolescents through individual therapy, highlighting the mourning processes they, no less than their parents, have to embark on. Chapter 12 draws on the conceptual framework offered in part I to address individual therapy with divorcing or divorced adults. It focuses on the defenses adults implement to block out painful feelings and examines the tightrope therapists must walk between attuning themselves to their patient's suffering and aligning with those defensive needs to block it out.

This book provides extensive clinical material. In order to maintain the confidentiality of the people I have worked with, I have altered many details, including some demographic information. I focus here on opposite-sex marriage only because I lack clinical information on same-sex couples. As we make strides in regard to marriage equality, I look forward to the opportunity to work with same-sex couples, too.

Part I

DIVORCE AND MOURNING

CHALLENGES FOR CHILDREN AND PARENTS

Chapter One

The Losses in Divorce

MARRIAGE AND HOPES FOR HEALING

To understand the psychological meanings of divorce, we first must consider some meanings of marriage. Picture for a moment the happiness of extended family members as they celebrate a wedding. Imagine the joy of the community as it participates in a ritual in which two people commit to a lifetime together, whatever hardships may arise. Weddings affirm our belief that two people can fall in love, stay in love, and take care of each other through the challenges that inevitably befall us. While rich in possibilities, intimacy challenges us. We all have suffered painful, even traumatic, experiences while growing up. Inevitably, then, all of us approach intimate relationships, including marriage, with fears (some conscious, others unconscious) that by committing to another person we will repeat our traumas—that the partner will fall ill or withdraw into depression as a parent did, for instance. For adults whose parents divorced, the search for intimacy is "haunted by powerful ghosts": the specter of failed relationships haunts each new relationship (Wallerstein, Lewis, and Blakeslee, 2000, p. xiii).

When a marriage (or any long-term, committed relationship) goes well, it can serve a number of functions psychologically, including:

- Providing a counterpoint to difficult childhood experience.
- Facilitating separation from the family of origin.
- Providing each partner with important *selfobject*[1] functions.

Marriage as a Counterpoint to Difficult Childhood Experience

Many of us have been inculcated with the belief that marriage is special, a buffer against life's hardships. Alongside troubling fears, then, stand ardent

3

hopes that marriage will be different: We will not *repeat* traumas but, instead, will find repair and healing.

> *Ms. Adams's father, though successful at work, suffered from bipolar disorder.*
> *When he went off medication, he raged at family members and, twice, as-*
> *saulted Ms. Adams's mother. Tough-minded and bright, Ms. Adams escaped*
> *into books, school and a few close girlfriends. At age eighteen, she fell in love*
> *with an ambitious, adventurous man, several years older than she. Overjoyed,*
> *Ms. Adams believed she finally had found her escape from the tumult of grow-*
> *ing up. At the same time, she awoke at night in an anxious sweat, wondering:*
> *Is this man really stable? Might he become mentally ill like my father?*

When a marriage (or any committed intimate relationship) remains stable and loving over time, it can provide assurance that our worst fears about the reemergence of early traumas—such as abandonment or abuse by a parent—are unwarranted.

A stable, loving relationship also can counteract lingering childhood feelings of smallness and inadequacy. In exploring childhood experience, psychoanalysts refer to the "primal scene." That term in its narrowest sense refers to children's witnessing parental sexual relations but more broadly to children's sense of smallness in relation to the parents and their awareness of adult prerogatives from which they are excluded. At the end of the day, parents go to their bedroom, shut the door, and engage in intimacies that do not include the child. Such feelings of being small and on the outside are recapitulated throughout childhood and adolescence, as in the case of a teenager suffering a painful humiliation when a longed-for boy or girl rejects his or her overtures (Person, 1986). In finding a partner and establishing a committed relationship, men and women often feel a triumphant sense that finally they have overcome painful childhood exclusion. Sexual intimacy, once the preserve of adults, now belongs to them, too. A loving marriage—or any committed loving relationship—can feel like a powerful step into the adult world.

Marriage and Separation-Individuation

A stable love relationship can facilitate the vital developmental process of separation-individuation, helping individuals establish a sense of self independent of the family of origin. Intimate sexual relationships in late adolescence and early adulthood facilitate women's ongoing development of a female identity (Barbour, 1981). For men, positive intimate relationships offer a venue in which they can re-work troubling childhood experiences and establish a more independent sense of self (Ehrlich, 1991). Lovers give up their ordinary sense of self and come to believe in what Person (1988) refers to as "the autonomous life of a new entity—the 'we' created by love" (p.

122). By transcending the boundaries of the self and identifying with the other, the lover is "no longer bound by old patterns, habits, and other rigidities of character" (p. 122). The new identity as a couple reverberates for each partner with images of important couples from the past, including the parents. Children can add richness and depth to a relationship as partners augment their identity as a couple by sharing parenting pleasures and challenges.

Selfobject Functions of Marriage

It is one role of parents to facilitate their children's development of a strong, vital self by serving as selfobjects: providing an "idealizing" function in which the developing child can bask in the glory of the admired parent and, in doing so, come to feel enhanced him- or herself; and a "mirroring" function in which the child basks in the experience of being the beloved apple of the parent's eye (Kohut, 1971, 1977). Both of these experiences, repeated over and over, are essential to the child's developing a coherent self that incorporates a sense of self-confidence and creative energy.

Parents inevitably falter in their capacities to provide idealizing and mirroring functions. Their lapses range from mild and intermittent (e.g., periods of anxious preoccupation) to catastrophic (e.g., a parent's major depression or chronic withdrawal). In response to these lapses in our childhoods, all of us engage in a lifelong search in relationships for the mirroring and idealizing we lacked growing up. The intensity of the quest correlates with the degree to which we suffered selfobject deficits growing up. We can see this quest in our sometimes frantic wishes to find others we can idealize, such as sports heroes and celebrities. We see it, too, in the hunger that drives all of us, to varying degrees, to be admired and valued by others.

Adults' hopes for healing in the adult love relationship emanate in part from wishes, often unconscious, to make up for deficits in the developing self: to bask in the glory of the idealized other and revel in being the apple of the other's eye. The "honeymoon phase" of romantic relationships, fueled by idealization of the relationship and the partner, fosters the hope that, indeed, an intimate relationship will heal old wounds. In stable, loving relationships, when partners gradually modulate unrealistic idealizations, they can take steady comfort in admiring the partner and also being admired.

WHEN A MARRIAGE COMES APART

When a marriage comes apart, each partner must deal with a range of emotional experiences, which include:

- The re-emergence of painful childhood experience.

- The loss of the experience of couplehood.
- The loss of the spouse's selfobject functions.

The Re-Emergence of Painful Childhood Experience

When a marriage falls apart, it has a cascading effect: Old traumas bubble to the surface, mixing and mingling inextricably with devastation at the current loss and, potentially, generating overwhelming emotional suffering. The partnership, instead of providing a longed-for buffer from life's harshness, has itself become harsh and, at its worst, painfully familiar. In addition to shattering a relationship, divorce can shatter hope.

> *Ms. Adams discovered gradually that her husband had serious mental health problems. While successful, he was recklessly squandering family resources on cocaine and strip clubs. Her devastation and bitterness reverberated with her agonizing childhood experience of dealing with her father's mental illness and its ravaging effects on her family. When Ms. Adams came for therapy, she appeared shell-shocked at the possibility that her worst fears were coming true: Her husband might be every bit as destructive as her father.*

When a marriage dissolves, adults who have delighted in being on the inside of an intimate couple are, catastrophically, on the outside again. This is especially true when one spouse finds a new partner. The experience of exclusion in the present reverberates unconsciously with long-forgotten childhood pain, compounding it. Divorcing or recently divorced people are prone to engage in repetitive, often frenzied sexual liaisons (Hetherington and Kelly, 2002) in an effort to ward off the pain of loneliness and to experience again, however briefly, the soothing quality of sexual intimacy. Often, they end up feeling even lonelier. While men who are narcissistically hurt by the end of a marriage can find affirmation of their sexual prowess in such encounters (Johnston, Roseby, and Kuehnle, 2009), their desperate activity prevents them from facing and learning to tolerate the experience of aloneness that is part of mourning.

The Loss of the Experience of Couplehood

Where the experience of the couple provides each partner with an identity separate from the family of origin, that identity dissolves when a marriage comes apart. Often, unresolved experiences of separation from the parents, buried away in the experience of couplehood, re-emerge around a divorce, so that extreme feelings of ambivalence, grief, and anxiety come pouring to the surface, even when a marriage has been unfulfilling (Rice and Rice, 1986). In addition, each partner must make the shift from being a member of a couple to being a "separated" or "divorced" individual. Johnston and Campbell (1988) describe the social dislocation that comes with divorce:

> The disintegration of the marriage involves the loss not only of a significant other but of a shared social and emotional reality, which in turn involves a loss or confusion of self-identity, a sense of anomie, or rootlessness. For these reasons, a common theme is a search for roots, for existential meaning, for a new sense of self and a sense of connection (p. 35).

The loss of the marital role can be experienced as a loss of status within a community, and creates anxiety about one's ability to create a new role (Rice and Rice, 1986).

The Loss of the Spouse's Selfobject Functions

When a marriage comes apart, each spouse loses the selfobject function that the other spouse provided. Instead of being admired and appreciated, each partner now feels shunned, disregarded, or disparaged; instead of basking in the pleasure of admiring the other, each partner now feels devastating disappointment or disdain. The loss of self-esteem is often excruciating. Feelings of inadequacy, worthlessness, and unattractiveness predominate. Rage, often kept in check in marriage by mutual idealization, comes pouring out and blocks out feelings of anguish at loss and a diminished sense of self. The loss of the spouse's selfobject functions resonates with earlier selfobject losses— a parent's withdrawal, for instance—increasing the sense of devastation. The frenzied search for new romantic/sexual partners that often follows a break-up can be understood in part as a desperate effort to replace lost selfobject functions.

THE MULTIPLE LOSSES IN DIVORCE

Mr. Berger was stunned by his wife's decision to end their marriage. A driven and accomplished businessman, Mr. Berger harbored the fantasy that he could control the world, a fantasy bolstered by business successes. Delighted by his wife's idealization of his accomplishments, he felt crushed as she became disillusioned with his lack of commitment to the family. Her decision to leave him shattered his fantasy of control and his enlivening experience of being admired, leaving him feeling small, inadequate, and ashamed. Alongside that terrible injury to his pride, Mr. Berger struggled to manage intense sorrow over losing a woman he had deeply loved. He engaged in a series of brief affairs that left him feeling even lonelier.

Mr. Berger's experience captures the multiple meanings of loss for adults as they divorce. Because his wife served soothing selfobject functions for him, bolstering his self-esteem, losing her meant losing important psychological *functions* she provided. Mr. Berger also was *attached* to his wife, appreciating her as a strong woman whose passion for the arts and child-rearing capacities he valued and appreciated. They had taken great pleasure in raising their children, and Mr. Berger especially cherished memories of family trips to his childhood home on the California coast. Thus, he was losing a person he had valued, relied on, and shared with. In addition, his wife's decision to end the marriage re-evoked painful childhood experiences of powerlessness and inadequacy when Mr. Berger had been rendered helpless by forces outside his control.

THE ROLE OF SPECIFIC CIRCUMSTANCES WHEN MARRIAGE ENDS

Divorce is rarely mutual, and the specific circumstances surrounding it make a huge difference. A gradual process of distancing tends to be less devastating than the sudden emergence of an affair, for example. Traumatic incidents at separations, such as violent confrontations or sudden exposure to a spouse's affair, can reverberate for years as divorced partners struggle to move on with their lives (Johnston and Campbell, 1988). Individuals with greater vulnerability to loss or narcissistic injury may be unable to bear the feelings associated with the breakup of a marriage. They can become severely depressed or locked into bitter recrimination; they may teem with a rage kept in check during the marriage by a denial of underlying frustration and disappointment.

Devastation is especially profound for those who are left. One study found that 25 percent of men involved in divorce had no idea their wives were thinking of leaving them (Hetherington and Kelly, 2002); their shock exacerbated their despair. Deciding to exit a marriage against the other person's wishes creates its own emotional turmoil, however, especially profound guilt—the more so when it recapitulates earlier similar experiences.

Ms. Chen finally ended her marriage after her first husband bounced in and out of treatment programs for cocaine abuse. She gradually stabilized a second marriage with a less turbulent man. However, she could not get her first husband out of her mind. Ms. Chen and her second husband sought marital treatment when he discovered that she was secretly channeling family money to fund her ex-husband's rehabilitation.

Ms. Chen described feeling responsible for her ex-husband's deterioration because she had ended the marriage. In the course of the marital therapy, she spoke with great sorrow about having left home for college while her father was slowly drinking himself to death, an experience that appeared to set the stage for her later absorption with a troubled man.

"Separation guilt" following a divorce can interfere with women's personal functioning and parenting (Baum, 2007). Yet, despite the burdens of guilt, spouses who leave often have the advantage of having worked through some of their feelings about a pending divorce ahead of time, so the end of the marriage is not as jarring for them as for the person left behind. At the same time, spouses that leave, focused on their wish to extricate themselves, may be more likely to deny the enormity of the loss (Emery, 2012). People who initiate divorce usually fail to anticipate just how arduous and challenging life post-divorce will be; while they long for a fresh start, divorce does not "wipe the slate clean" as they had hoped (Wallerstein and Blakeslee, 1989, p. 4).

NOTE

1. Selfobject, the central concept in psychoanalytic self psychology, refers to "an object that a person experiences as incompletely separated from himself and that serves to maintain his sense of self" (Socarides and Stolorow, 1984, p. 105).

Chapter Two

Mourning

How can you say goodbye to someone with whom you have shared a bed, daily routines, tender expressions of love, long-term goals, vacations, the negotiating of life's ups and downs? In the case of divorcing parents, how can you say goodbye to someone with whom you have raised children?

Mourning, a goodbye process, is essential for all of us throughout our lives. We need to mourn the losses of beloved others, the passage of time, our limitations and failings and the limitations and failings of the people around us. While a wish to move through losses and embrace new opportunities might propel us forward, change brings confrontation with the unknown, which is frightening. "Relinquishment of the familiar" (Steiner, 2005) often is the hardest part of moving forward because it challenges our natural inclination to cling to the status quo, even when it is unsatisfying. Mourning can be defined as:

> . . . the conglomerate of favorable processes that develops in the face of loss. It includes acceptance of reality and readaptation to it. Mourning means acceptance of one's perpetual vulnerability to loss and betrayal, as well as to one's own limitations and to the finality of life (Kogan, 2007, p. 1).

Mourning "permits us to relinquish attachments and attitudes that have lost their realistic usefulness, thus facilitating growth and development" (Kogan, 2007, p. 1). According to Thomas Ogden (2002), a contemporary psychoanalyst, its central feature is dealing with emotional pain: "living with it, symbolising it for oneself, and doing psychological work with it" (p. 777).

Mourning involves *tolerating* painful affects over time: bearing core feelings of sorrow, regret, hurt, shame, and disappointment long enough to move through them. In doing so, the mourner must overcome his or her defenses against the pain of loss. Psychoanalysts use the word "metabolize" to de-

11

scribe this gradual process of working and reworking emotionally laden experiences so that they are no longer so raw and dissonant. Metabolizing feelings related to loss involves being fully aware of them and allowing oneself to connect them to other experiences of loss and separation. While movement toward resolution of painful feelings in successful mourning is never complete, it is significant, and gradually takes the edge off difficult feelings.

Because our minds naturally recoil at the idea that someone we have loved is no longer with us (or no longer wants to be with us), we may deny that reality. Mourning the loss of a loved one, then, includes dealing with harsh reality, what Ogden (2002) describes as the "hard edge of recognition of one's inability to undo the fact of the loss of the object" (p. 775). We must gradually come to terms, in other words, with the limits of our powers, including our inability to fully control the most important aspects of our lives.

Recent psychoanalytic writings on loss and mourning (Aragno, 2003; Deutsch, 2011; Gaines, 1997) focus on the maintenance of the tie to the lost person as part of the mourning process. Gaines argues that in mourning, alongside detachment, we create a sense of continuity that affirms the emotional connection to the person we have lost. In regard to divorce, for instance, people may adopt admired qualities of a once-beloved ex-spouse or, over time, come to value qualities in a child that remind them of the former spouse. The creation of continuity has a "bittersweet" quality, according to Gaines. It serves both as a reminder of the person that has been lost as well as providing a balm for the pain of loss. Detachment and continuity can be viewed as the opposite of clinging to the lost person because both acknowledge loss.

TASKS OF MOURNING

Hagman (1995), a psychoanalyst who writes extensively on mourning, suggests that mourning can be framed as meeting a series of emotional and environmental demands. He concurs with Ogden that recognizing reality is critical to mourning and identifies additional tasks:

- Expressing, modulating and containing grief.
- Coping with environmental and social change.
- Transforming the psychical relationship with the lost object.
- Restoring the self internally and within the social milieu.

These overlapping tasks place enormous emotional demands on the mourner, often for years. The intrapsychic tasks of integrating the reality of loss and managing grief strain the internal resources of even well-adapted individuals.

Loss of a relationship has different personal meanings, which bear heavily on mourning. A person who feels betrayed or exploited, for instance, may infuse the mourning process with hatred or fantasies of retaliation. Another may experience the excruciating recapitulation of childhood losses that compound grief exponentially. Aragno (2003), citing the groundbreaking work of Bowlby on separation and loss in childhood, writes, "All genuine mourning reaches deeply archaic layers of the personality, but for those with lesions from real early loss or separation traumas, the current loss reopens profoundly embedded scars" (p. 450). The capacity to manage grief depends on various factors, including culture, a person's capacity to tolerate painful affects, and the presence of significant people in one's environment who can bear difficult feelings and thus facilitate mourning.

Divorcing partners, especially a spouse who is left, often manifest frantic efforts at denial. Absorbing painful reality is a gradual process that proceeds in fits and starts—confrontation, denial in the face of unbearable feelings, then confrontation once again. Struggling against mourning can serve an adaptive function, at least for a time, allowing a person to fend off despair (Kogan, 2007). However, difficulties embarking on a mourning process also can contribute to the confusion around boundaries that researchers observe in the first few years post-divorce. About 25 percent of adults in the midst of divorcing believed their marriages still could be saved through hard work (Doherty et al., 2011). At two months post-divorce, 15 percent of couples reported that they still had sexual relations; three fourths of the women and two thirds of the men said they would call the ex-spouse first in an emergency (Hetherington and Kelly, 2002). While calling on an ex-spouse may be adaptive in some circumstances—for instance, when a person has no other resources available and desperately needs help—reliance on the ex-spouse often signals difficulties disengaging from the ex-spouse and creating new relationships.

PARTICULAR CHALLENGES OF MOURNING DIVORCE

Mourners, even while coping with profound internal challenges, have to manage the social environment, including massive life changes wrought by the loss. They must negotiate the shift from being a husband or wife to a single person. Divorcing parents must come to terms with moving from being part of a parental unit to being a "single parent." In the midst of their upheaval, parents must attend—physically, financially, emotionally—to children in the throes of *their* divorce-related distress; dealing with a beloved child's suffering strains bereft parents even more. The intersection between parents' mourning and children's emotional needs after divorce frames many of the challenges that children and parents face when a marriage comes apart (see chapter 4).

Loving feelings and happy memories do not vanish when a marriage falls apart, even though, in the midst of a breakup, spouses might bury tenderness away. When a marriage goes sour, loving feelings become inextricably bound up with sadness over loss—a wrenching testament to the painful reality that what was good is gone. To mourn the end of a marriage, a person must be willing and able to bear the sorrow that comes with recalling happy moments. After a divorce, too, one cannot simply turn off concern, curiosity, and investment. Mourning a divorce, then, includes allowing oneself to be aware of how painful it feels that the spouse is creating a separate life that includes relationships and activities to which one no longer has access. Awareness of sadness at this turn of events contrasts with a defensive need to effect a stance of nonchalance or precipitate unpleasant arguments with the ex-spouse that block out sadness and forestall a goodbye.

Bitter Entanglement with the Former Partner as a Defense Against Mourning

> *Ms. Drew and Mr. Drew, high school sweethearts who married at twenty-one, squabbled for the first few months after their separation following a ten-year marriage. Ms. Drew flared angrily at each exchange of the children, accusing Mr. Drew of being negligent as a parent. Mr. Drew retorted that Ms. Drew was a "pain in the ass" and needed to leave him alone. Their anger obscured overt signs of sadness over the reality that their relationship, which once had a fairy-tale quality, had fallen apart.*

Bitter entanglement with an ex-spouse that does not resolve is a signal of stuck or failed mourning: an angry locking in with another person (in actuality or in one's mind), as opposed to bearing disappointment and sorrow and gradually moving through it. While such entanglement is most prominent when conflict is high—it might be viewed as the essence of high-conflict divorce—it plays a role in all divorces as two people struggle to manage painful feelings catalyzed by the extraordinarily hard task of disengaging from an intimate attachment.

Hopes for Reconciliation

In contrast to death (with the exception of suicide), at least one person in a couple *chooses* divorce, which adds layers of complexity to the emotional experience for rejecter and rejected alike. The fact that divorce potentially is reversible also complicates reality; hopes for reconciliation can live on for both children and adults. Some families pretend the divorce never happened by interacting as they did prior to the divorce. Such an approach can make the already difficult task of mourning harder for all family members.

> *For two years after their divorce, Ms. Elwood and Mr. Elwood shared Thanksgiving and Christmas. While they did it, they said, for the sake of the children, whose holidays they did not wish to ruin, they came to realize they were simply forestalling the inevitable. They would need to bear the loneliness that would come with experiencing these once special family events without each other's presence.*

Ms. Elwood and Mr. Elwood had the maturity to recognize that they were having trouble getting over the end of their marriage and moving on with their lives. In that context, they understood that continued intimate contact was counterproductive. While it may be possible for ex-spouses to share occasions such as holidays, it can become problematic if parents fail to reflect honestly on their motivations for doing so and deny any negative impact on their children (e.g., stirring unrealistic hopes for reconciliation).

By contrast, some former partners wish to place as much distance as possible between themselves and the other person when their relationship ends. Divorcing parents, however, usually *have* to interact with each other, often for years. Each interaction can stir longing, sadness, and outrage. They often ask poignantly: How am I supposed to get over a spouse that I have to see or talk to every few days? While contact with the ex-spouse can be excruciating, it also can briefly ameliorate devastation at the separation and stimulate wishes for reconciliation that interfere with coming to terms with the end of the relationship (Jacobson and Jacobson, 1987).

The Challenging Presence of Children

The presence of children adds additional challenges for parents who are mourning the end of a marriage. Creating and raising children together represents the culmination of their intimacy for many couples. When the marriage comes apart, the children's presence becomes a painful reminder of what each spouse has lost. In addition, children often are reminders of the ex-spouse in their physical appearance, specific gestures, or other characteristics.

> *James, age ten, brilliant and quirky, shares many traits with his father, an engineering professor. Gifted at math and absentminded like his father, James drifts into daydreams about cars that fly and truck engines the size of milk cartons. James's mother found these qualities endearing when the parents were together. Now his idiosyncracies evoke angry thoughts about her ex-husband, whose quirkiness and lack of social skills contributed to the marriage's deterioration.*

Many young adults, in reflecting on their childhood experience of divorce, recalled their parents remarking disparagingly that the child's behaviors reminded them of the other parent (Marquardt, 2005).

Unresolved Issues from the Marriage Itself

Often, a person's difficulty coming to terms with disappointing features of the spouse during the marriage spill over into difficulties with mourning when the relationship ends.

> *Ms. Hall, an apologetic, guilt-ridden woman spent fourteen years married to a man who, by all accounts, was paranoid. He frequently disparaged her, bugged her cell phone, and kept a careful journal of what he termed her "cumulative transgressions." For years, Ms. Hall denied her husband's psychopathology, mainly by blaming herself for his behavior. But finally, at the behest of friends and family, she filed for divorce.*

For several years following the divorce, Ms. Hall anxiously wondered if she had made a mistake by leaving. When her husband angrily blamed her for the divorce, she guiltily concurred that she was responsible because she had left. For brief moments, she could recognize that her ex-husband's paranoia provided ample justification for her decision, but she still found the reality of his mental illness unbearable and quickly reverted to blaming herself.

> *Mr. Ives watched in sadness as his wife of fifteen years became increasingly depressed and enraged. Too anxious to leave the house, she spent the days watching television, then blew up at him for not attending to domestic chores when he returned from work. Mr. Ives thought about leaving for years but felt overcome by a sense of guilt and responsibility. His wife's angry accusations reverberated with his own guilty conscience. Eventually, however, becoming depressed himself, he initiated a divorce.*

Like Ms. Hall, Mr. Ives struggled for years with a debilitating sense of guilt that he had abandoned his spouse. He did not allow himself the pleasure of seeking a new relationship until four years after the divorce.

OTHER PERSPECTIVES ON MOURNING THE LOSSES IN DIVORCE

Robert Emery (2012), a prominent writer and researcher on divorce, focuses on the "cycles of grief" that follow divorce, noting that grief in divorce often is overlooked, instead of encouraged. He believes the lack of finality in divorce, especially as represented by the presence of children, interferes with grieving. His "cyclical theory" of grief argues that people cycle back and forth among the conflicting emotions of love, anger, and sadness—that is, because divorce is not irrevocable, divorced adults revisit these feelings as their hopes for reunion are repeatedly awakened, then dashed. Emery suggests that some adults get "stuck" on one emotion but most people, over time, experience the full cycle of emotions. Consistent with the approach to mourning that I articulate, Emery suggests that "sooner or later, it seems, you have to deal with the pain" (p. 45). In other words, in order to progress through cycles of grief, divorcing adults need to recognize and experience their underlying sadness.

Nehami Baum (2004, 2004a, 2006, 2006a, 2007), an Israeli social worker who writes from a psychoanalytic perspective, focuses on intrapsychic aspects to mourning divorce, but also notes the salience of interpersonal variables, such as hostility from the ex-spouse, which can slow the mourning process for both partners. Baum (2006a) observes that the ability to integrate the loved and hated aspects of the former spouse and the marriage is key to adjusting emotionally to divorce over time. She asserts that the accentuation of the negative immediately following divorce serves an adaptive function by mitigating guilt for the leaver and narcissistic injury for the spouse who is left and also helping to counteract the wish to reconcile that stems from separation anxiety.

Judith Wallerstein (1989) sees mourning as an important psychological task for divorcing adults. She writes:

> Each ex-partner must first acknowledge the loss and mourn the dreams and hopes that were never fully realized and never will be fully realized. It is important to cry, for only crying reduces anger to human size. And only by mourning can a person regain or maintain perspective on what was lost. And only by mourning will the adults be able to close the door and move on. Even the most miserable marriage embodied some expectation of a better life, companionship, love, and esteem, and although no tears may be shed for the lost partner, the symbolic meaning of the marriage should be put to rest with gentleness (p. 279).

Consistent with my views, Wallerstein here posits that the *meaning* of marriage is critical in the months and years that follow divorce and that failure to mourn presents dangers for divorcing adults, such as paralyzing longing for the ex-spouse. It also interferes with parents' ability to deal with their children's underlying hurt and sorrow, which has long-term implications for their children's mental health. Wallerstein suggests that, along with mourning, divorced adults must "reclaim" themselves by relinquishing the connections to the former spouse and entering unencumbered into new relationships or ventures. I would view that "reclaiming" not as separate from mourning, but as the outcome of a constructive mourning process.

Mavis Hetherington, a prominent divorce researcher, suggests that ex-spouses employ "divorce scripts" to explain why their marriages fell apart (Hetherington and Kelly, 2002). Other than ex-spouses who lock into endless recrimination, former partners continuously revise and update these scripts. Many divorced adults move from construing themselves as noble, long-suffering victims to generating more measured, balanced accounts that take heed of their own contributions to marital problems. While the researchers use the language of "letting go" rather than frame these shifts in terms of mourning, I would frame them as the culmination of a mourning process whereby people have been able to bear the feelings that arise when they give up a defensive stance of blaming the spouse and own their contribution to the failure of the marriage. Hetherington and Kelly determine that alterations in a divorce script occur over three to four years—a span that speaks to the gradual nature of the mourning process.

DEFENSES IN THE FACE OF LOSS

Understanding the defenses of divorcing individuals helps to illuminate why some progress through a constructive mourning process while others get mired in acrimony. In the face of painful feelings associated with separation and loss, all of us implement defenses in pursuit of emotional equilibrium, and for the most part we do so unconsciously and seamlessly. Many divorcing adults resort to emotional distancing and fury to fend off sorrow and shame. Others turn to acting-out behaviors, such as substance use and frenetic sexual activity. Defenses serve to address internal conflict—for instance, intolerable guilt over loving and hating the same person. Simultaneously, defenses influence our interactions with the world around us—for instance, when we become withdrawn in the face of sad feelings, we become emotionally unavailable to others.

Based on a longitudinal study of men's adaptation and failed adaptation in their careers and intimate relationships, George Vaillant (1977), a psychiatrist at Harvard Medical School, outlined a hierarchy of defenses in terms of the degree to which they facilitate adaptation.

- *Psychotic defenses*—for example, delusional projection, distortion—alter reality for the user, though, by definition, the user does not know this (think of trying to reason with someone with a paranoid delusion). Psychotic defenses appear "crazy" to the beholder.
- *Immature defenses*—for example, projection, acting out—are common in adolescents and people with addictions and personality disorders, who use them as a way to resolve conflicts catalyzed by either the presence or loss of other people. Vaillaint observes, and this bears on the high-conflict

divorce, "reason, interpretation and threats fail to alter immature defenses" (p. 83).

- *Neurotic defenses*—for example, intellectualization, repression—are much less likely to alter external reality. They come across as quirks and are readily amenable to intervention. According to Vaillant, they are used primarily to manage intrapsychic conflict.
- *Mature defenses*—for example, humor and sublimation—successfully integrate reality, relationships, and private feelings. They come across as "convenient virtues" (p. 385).

In contrast to a person who uses *immature* or *psychotic* defenses (see chapter 3), people who employ *neurotic* and *mature* defenses can much more readily mourn the losses in divorce because these defenses allow at least some access to underlying feelings of shame, sadness, and guilt. People who write sad songs about a breakup or write an advice column on dealing with divorce—examples of sublimation—have integrated sorrow effectively into daily life. People who use self-deprecating humor to describe their contributions to the demise of a marriage have found a socially acceptable way to talk about a wrenching topic.

In order to mourn, a person does not need to stay immersed in sadness, shame, and guilt all of the time, but must rely on defenses that allow for *significant* access to these painful affects.

> *Mr. Flynn entered therapy because he felt he felt emotionally overwhelmed by his decision to end his marriage. He alternated between periods of relief that his difficult marriage finally was over and bouts of sadness that his dream of a stable, loving marriage had fallen apart. At times, in almost celebratory expressions of relief, Mr. Flynn found respite from grief. Other times, when he allowed himself to remember the happy times when he and his wife first fell in love, he wept. While he initially focused in therapy on his wife's disappointing qualities, Mr. Flynn quickly came to reflect on his withdrawal from her during the marriage, which he believed contributed to her unhappiness.*

While Mr. Flynn needed relief at times, his defensive movement away from grief was adaptive in that it did not contribute to escalating tensions, in contrast to immature and psychotic defenses. His defenses also were flexible enough that he could return to mourning, which included thoughtful (albeit painful) reflections on his contributions to the end of his marriage.

In the face of divorce, some people temporarily regress in the types of defenses they use. Those who are ordinarily able to mobilize neurotic and mature defenses may shift into periods of acting out or projection in response to overwhelming sadness and anger. Baum (2006a) suggests that such regression may serve an adaptive function immediately after a divorce by enabling a self-protective denial of sorrow about losing the spouse. Over time, though, in order to move ahead, it becomes necessary to mobilize more mature defenses that allow the integration of sorrow.

CONSTRUCTIVE MOURNING

Constructive mourning involves overlapping tasks: accepting our own and our ex-spouse's flaws, giving up what was good in the marriage, and reworking earlier losses. Because marriage has idiosyncratic meanings for each person, the tasks involved in mourning the end of a marriage vary. When a marriage ends with bitter arguing, as one example, mourning includes gradually giving up resentful blaming of the ex-spouse for the arguments and acknowledging some responsibility for hurting the ex-spouse through angry outbursts and empathic lapses. In following such a path, mourners gradually accept their flaws and the fact that their flaws hurt people they love. Mourning includes bearing disappointment in the ex-spouse for those limitations that helped bring about the marital impasse. Mourning also means gradually coming to terms with the loss of a spouse's selfobject functions: giving up how good we once felt in admiring the spouse and how his or her admiration of us was enhancing. Ideally, according to Gaines (1997), the mourner over time creates a sense of continuity with the person he or she has lost—a way of retaining elements of a relationship that had once been so central.

Mourning as a Developmental Step

Mourning, by allowing greater attunement to difficult features of reality, constitutes a positive developmental step that has significant repercussions for relationships. Recognizing and accepting our own problematic behaviors, for instance, allows for the possibility of changing them and also connecting empathically with the ex-spouse's perspective and justified disappointment in us, as opposed to engaging only in blame. Taking heed of one's own destructiveness and the destructiveness of the former partner brings guilt and disappointment but, eventually, relief.

> *Mr. Berger, the businessman described earlier, thrived in being the apple of his wife's eye. When she shifted to harsh criticism and disappointment in him, he felt crushed. In the months following the divorce, Mr. Berger grieved the loss of her admiration of him. Gradually, as he came to accept her changed views of him, which included his acknowledgment that he disappointed her by refusing to talk about their marital problems and working too much, he was ready to seek a new relationship.*

When divorce represents a repetition of earlier losses or traumas, constructive mourning includes working through these earlier experiences in addition to the loss of the marriage.

Ms. Adams, the woman whose father had an often untreated bipolar disorder, was heartbroken to discover that her husband was a lot like her disturbed father, as opposed to being the longed-for antidote to her troubled childhood. In mourning the loss of her marriage, including the fantasy that she could make up for the sorrows of her childhood, Ms. Adams also mourned the lack of a healthy father she had so desperately wanted.

For both Mr. Berger and Ms. Adams, the mourning process around divorce was arduous (see chapter 12).

SOME OUTCOMES OF CONSTRUCTIVE MOURNING

Moving on Productively with One's Life

While the first few years post-divorce are painful and confusing for everyone involved—including longings for the ex-spouse and severe logistical challenges—many people move beyond those difficult experiences to create viable and enriching lives. In their longitudinal study, for instance, Hetherington and Kelly (2002) found that the majority of women viewed their divorces as a positive event in their lives: "It had freed them from a dying relationship, created opportunities for self-discovery, and exposed them to the satisfactions of work" (p. 97).

Forgiveness of the Ex-Spouse

Genuine forgiveness signals that successful mourning has taken place. The opposite of bitterness, it encompasses forgiving ourselves for own contributions to the end of the marriage as well as forgiving the spouse. Achieving forgiveness of the spouse following divorce has been negatively correlated with being depressed and angry and positively correlated with feeling a sense of "existential well-being" (Rye et al., 2004). However, that conclusion does not consider that the *capacity* to forgive depends on certain psychological strengths that divorcing adults bring to post-divorce adjustment, precisely those strengths that both enable and derive from mourning.

Non-Acrimonious Interactions with the Ex-Spouse

When significant mourning has occurred, former marital partners can interact without overwhelming distress, or, at the least, find ways to modulate it so it does not infiltrate interactions in toxic ways. Hetherington and Kelly (2002) found that the relationship with the ex-spouse, which played such a major role for the first few years post-divorce, steadily faded in importance for most divorced couples. This is critical for divorced parents who share the care of children.

Over the course of two years, tensions abated between Ms. Drew and Mr. Drew, the former high school sweethearts. They stopped bickering at exchanges of the children and were able to negotiate changes in the parenting arrangement with minimal tension. Ms. Drew was able to communicate to Mr. Drew that she appreciated his flexibility with the parenting arrangement. He was able to let her know that he appreciated the quality of her parenting.

The vast majority (about 80 percent) of divorcing parents are able to reach successful resolution of custody issues without the need of a neutral third party associated with the court (Macoby and Mnookin, 1992), suggesting at least some capacity to disengage.

Parents who navigate divorce without undue turbulence and co-parent comfortably often do not come to the attention of mental health professionals. They may seek help in a non-adversarial forum—for instance, by seeking a brief consultation with a divorce expert in advance of the divorce to discuss how to limits stressors for their children. Emery (2012) describes how former spouses "renegotiate" their marital relationship, a process in which they move from being married lovers to, essentially, business partners in co-parenting. This passage reflects a constructive mourning process in which former spouses come to accept that the special intimacies of their prior relationship no longer apply. While longings may arise and old hurts may rear their heads, individuals who have successfully renegotiated their relationship manage these feelings internally—that is, regulate them sufficiently so they do not spill over into negotiations with the ex-spouse. Pedro-Carroll (2010) and Johnston and Campbell (1988) explain that divorcing parents can establish a businesslike mode of interacting by maintaining clear boundaries and communicating respectfully, essentially removing intense emotions from their interactions.

Although Emery (2012) suggests that the goal of renegotiating the marital relationship is not only to avoid becoming angry when the ex-spouse calls but to get to the point where one does not even recognize his or her voice, such a degree of detachment is probably impossible unless one is fooling oneself or rigidly disavowing feelings about the ex-spouse so they are no longer available to consciousness. Because mourning is unlikely ever to be complete, *some degree* of anger and sadness is inevitable and appropriate if one has loved and then lost a person, even after many years. Assuming that sadness and anger are inevitable byproducts of divorce, critical questions remain: How well does a person manage anger and sadness? Is a person moving through difficult feelings such that these feelings are attenuated? And, critical for children: How does parents' management of difficult feelings in the post-divorce period bear on their capacity to attend thoughtfully to their children?

Chapter Three

Failures of Mourning

WHY ARE SOME PEOPLE UNABLE TO MOURN?

Barriers to successful mourning are myriad. They include a history of child-hood experiences of trauma and deprivation and, as a manifestation of these, chronic difficulties in the ability to modulate intense affects. Failure to mourn early experiences of loss and rejection make mourning in adulthood difficult if not impossible because current losses reverberate with old losses, magnifying them.

Psychoanalytic Views

Psychoanalysts have long been interested in how people deal with loss—less in the events surrounding loss than the *meanings* of loss for a particular person. In his groundbreaking paper "Mourning and Melancholia," Sigmund Freud (1917) addressed a vexing clinical conundrum: Why do some people manage to mourn, albeit with great psychic pain, while others get stuck in "melancholia" (what we might think of today as serious depression, replete with outrage and self-recrimination)? Freud was interested in loss by death, but also paid attention to "real slight or disappointment coming from the loved person" (p. 249). He observed that people whose "object choice has been effected on a narcissistic basis" (p. 249) are unable to mourn adequate-ly. Instead of mourning the loss of a person—a painstaking process of re-engaging all of the "memories and expectations" bound up with that per-son—they identify with the person they have lost. Freud was mainly con-cerned with intrapsychic phenomena, but addressed briefly the difficult inter-personal qualities of individuals who are entrapped in melancholia.

Since Freud, psychoanalysts have written extensively on loss, mourning, and failures of mourning, refining and expanding Freud's original ideas.

Much of the literature focuses on the impact of early childhood experiences on the later capacity to mourn. Melanie Klein (1940) argues that the greatest danger to constructive mourning comes when the mourner turns his or her hatred against the lost loved person. Bowlby (1963) emphasizes unconscious reproach and unconscious yearning toward the lost object as central impediments to a constructive mourning process. More recent contributions focus on the harmful impact on adult mourning of severe early trauma (e.g., Kogan, 2007, Krystal, 1991) and early difficulties in separation-individuation (Settlage, 2007). Thomas Ogden (2002), an important contemporary psychoanalytic theorist, in a brilliant explication of "Mourning and Melancholia," highlights the central role of narcissistic attachments in Freud's paper and clarifies that people with narcissistic attachments are unable to relate to others as distinct individuals with needs of their own. Because of this inability to experience others as fully separate, the melancholic is "unable to face the full impact of the reality of loss" and successfully disengage from the lost object (p. 775).

The writings of Heinz Kohut (1971, 1977) offer an especially helpful framework for thinking about the narcissistic vulnerabilities that impede constructive mourning. For most divorcing people, the need to move on and find new sources of gratification and support eventually holds sway and propels a mourning process. While painful and often grueling, it is possible. However, for acutely narcissistically vulnerable people, who lacked essential mirroring and idealizing experiences in childhood, the spouse not only provided critical selfobject *functions* as part of a complex relationship but, in essence, *became* a selfobject. Vitality, even psychic survival, depended on the other.

A person who relies upon others primarily as selfobjects experiences them in terms of the functions they provide rather than recognize them as distinct individuals with their own needs and volition. Because the selfobject is felt to be indistinguishable from the self and within omnipotent control, the leaving person's decision to leave is felt to be unacceptable and inexplicable. The person who is left thinks (and truly believes): It is impossible that you would wish to leave if I wish you to stay. Confronted with intolerable helplessness in the face of separation, the person seeks to reestablish fantasied omnipotent control.

> *Ms. Green was the product of a bleak childhood with minimal parenting and few friends. When she married, she imagined her new husband would turn her life around. In interaction with this intelligent man with a lively sense of humor, Ms. Green felt alive and, for the first time in her life, imagined a life without loneliness and depression. Her husband, though, dashed her hopes for a fulfilling life. Increasingly aware of her difficulties in being intimate, he gradually withdrew from her and eventually told her he wanted a divorce. Ms. Green, incredulous, told him flatly, "you cannot leave me."*

People with acute narcissistic vulnerability often have a different agenda in response to loss than those who are motivated to push through a mourning process: to hold tight to the other person as long as possible in hopes of reconstituting the relationship or, alternatively, punishing the person. In addition, the narcissistically vulnerable individual, prone to feeling shamed and inadequate in the face of separation and loss, tends to insist on maintaining a conscious experience of a grandiose and superior self (Gorkin, 1984).

> *Ms. Green, beside herself with rage that her husband was choosing to end their marriage, vowed he would never get a penny from her. She swore she was by far the superior parent and declared he would never have primary care of their son, even though he had been the son's primary caregiver up until then. Ms. Green hired the most aggressive attorney she could find and began a ferocious court battle that lasted for years.*

While the emergence of aggression is typical around a divorce, the inability to modulate aggression over time can be viewed as a hallmark of pathological mourning (Gorkin, 1984).

THE HIGH-CONFLICT DIVORCE AS A FAILURE OF MOURNING

Demographics and Definitions

Research show that 51 percent of parents report "negligible" conflict over custody and visitation issues, 24 percent report "mild" conflict, 10 percent report "substantial" conflict, and 15 percent "intense" conflict (Macoby and Mnookin, 1992). High-conflict divorces, although a relatively small proportion of domestic relation cases, take up about 90 percent of family courts' attention (Coates and Fieldstone, 2008).

The concept of "high conflict" has been ambiguous and vague in the literature. While acknowledging it is hard to define because families differ, Coates and Fieldstone offer the following description: "These parents engage in intractable conflict that is ongoing and unresolved and that intensifies after the divorce or separation rather than diminishing" (p. 9). The parties "litigate and re-litigate over minor and inconsequential issues generated by their own need to control or punish each other, often obstructing access to the children" (p. 9). Demby (2009) cites the centrality of hatred in the high-conflict divorce, which is prominent in people with narcissistic or borderline personality disorders. He points to the persistent tension in these individuals between wanting to harm or destroy the partner and at the same time desperately needing that person.

An Example of the High-Conflict Divorce: The James Parents

What not to do ...

*After a thirteen-year marriage marred by loud arguing and occasional shov-
ing matches, Dr. James and Mr. James divorced. Dr. James accused her
husband of being an unfit parent because he watched online pornography
(which he denied) and showed no capacity for empathy. She argued he should
have limited contact with their daughter, Leah, 9, and no overnights. In turn,
Mr. James argued that his wife had a serious personality disorder, a diagnosis
he claimed was proffered by their marital therapist (which Dr. James denied).*

*Dr. James and Mr. James spent tens of thousands of dollars on attorney
fees battling over the intricacies of their divorce agreement. Their attorneys,
as embittered and polarized as their clients, virtually snarled at each other in
court. A parenting coordinator, appointed by the court to help them resolve
conflicts, threatened to resign when Dr. James stated she was no longer willing to sit in the same room as her ex-husband, forestalling constructive mediation.*

*Two years post-divorce: The parents' new spouses have gotten drawn into
the disputes, furiously accusing each other of meddling. Mr. James and Dr.
James's new husband almost come to blows at Leah's soccer game, mortifying
her. The court has ordered that transitions between homes take place at school
after the parents descend into ugly name-calling. Dr. James has threatened to
talk to Leah about Mr. James's use of pornography. He in turn tells Leah that
her mother is a "self-absorbed bitch." Leah has become increasingly withdrawn and depressed.*

*Four years post-divorce: Dr. James and Mr. James, their conflict unabat-
ed, almost come to blows in the court hallway. The judge, despite her reputa-
tion for calm, angrily lectures the parents and their attorneys for taking up the
court's time. Leah, besieged by her parents' feuding and weary of negotiating
between two households, abruptly declares that her father is right about her
mother's "bitchiness." She refuses to return to her mother's home. Dr. James
calls the police.*

Divorce by definition means ending a relationship. However, four years post-
divorce Dr. James and Mr. James appear as *fully engaged* as they were
during their marriage. People around them have been drawn into the dispute.
Their child is overwhelmed. Helpers throw their hands up in despair. Dr. and
Mr. James, in contrast to parents who successfully "renegotiate" their relationships and become business-like in interacting, feud about every aspect of
their child's care and are unable to disentangle emotionally.

The Contributions of Jan Johnston and her Co-Authors to an Understanding of the High-Conflict Divorce

Jan Johnston and her co-authors (Johnston and Campbell, 1988; Johnston,
Roseby, and Kuehnle, 2009) describe high-conflict divorces as involving
parents who remain distrustful of each other, argue frequently, and undermine each other's roles as parents. Domestic violence is reported in one half

to three fourths of couples who litigate custody. The authors observe that about two thirds of individuals who get mired in high conflict have Axis II diagnoses, including paranoid, borderline, and schizoid personality disorders.

Johnston and Campbell argue that the inability to resolve disputes derives from an interplay of problems on three levels: intrapsychic, interactional, and the larger group. In regard to intrapsychic phenomena, the authors divide feuding parents into two categories: those with reactivated trauma and those with chronic difficulties with separation and loss (which corresponds to Ogden's description of individuals with narcissistic attachments). They cite problems with mourning in the first group: "These are parents who are basically intact . . . who have a specific difficulty in mourning the loss of a real, psychologically separate loved one" (p. 104). Those in the second group lack adequate psychic structure to mourn and often lock into custody disputes in a desperate effort to maintain ties to the spouse. That effort reflects an inability to tolerate feelings of loss, sadness, and loneliness.

Johnston and Campbell cite the central role of threats to self-esteem and self-integrity, observing that many participants in ongoing litigation seek to bolster a sense of self in response to excruciating feelings of humiliation and shame. In discussing the interactional level, they focus on two types of couples who have trouble disengaging: couples with highly idealized positive views of each other and couples with "extremely negative polarized" views of each other. On a broader level, they cite the role of "tribal warfare" in which others around the divorcing pair are drawn into the fray.

Mismatch in Degrees of Psychological Disturbance in High-Conflict Divorces

While the literature tends to focus on couples with equally pronounced, interlocking psychological problems, high-conflict divorces do not always involve partners with the same level of psychological disturbance. In some situations, one spouse contends accurately that the other has serious character pathology or is mentally ill and caused most of the difficulties in the marriage and post-separation. In such situations the more psychologically intact parent chose a more troubled partner for complicated neurotic reasons. Often, their dysfunctional marriages contrast sharply with other domains of their lives—work, parenting, friendships—where they function well, sometimes exceptionally so. Tragically, even when one partner seeks a calm resolution to a marriage, the other partner can make that impossible, as was the case with the divorces below.

> *Mr. Kuhn was drawn to his wife by the fantasy that he could rescue this depressed woman and, through his love, enliven her. This fantasy derived from his childhood experience of being helpless to animate his depressed mother and his wish to reverse the pain of that experience. Mr. Kuhn had a number of*

strengths, including the capacity to be a loving, stable father. He was taken aback at his wife's retaliatory rage around his decision to initiate a divorce. He earnestly proposed mediation in the futile hope that they could move through it with minimal conflict.

Ms. Lee, a kind, thoughtful but self-abnegating and guilt-ridden woman, got involved at age nineteen with an older man whom she saw as brilliant and charming and who she imagined would rescue her from her dysfunctional family. During their courtship, Ms. Lee denied the seriousness of his brief flashes of fury and fits of jealousy, attributing them to her inability to keep him happy. Within a few years after they wed, her husband had taken over their social calendar and finances and criticized Ms. Lee for being "stupid" and "boring." When she finally recognized that she could not influence his chronic outrage, Ms. Lee mobilized the courage to initiate a divorce. Her husband, furious, initiated a court action to gain custody of their toddler daughter, even though he had barely played a role in her care.

Mr. Morales, a successful executive, burdened for years by excruciating self-doubt and guilt, decided to divorce his wife after she suffered two psychotic breaks that required hospitalization and then refused to take psychiatric medications. He was convinced, correctly, that she would be unable to care for their school-aged son without exposing him to danger. When Mr. Morales sought full custody, his wife fought him tooth and nail, initiating repeated court battles and accusing Mr. Morales of outrageous transgressions. Eventually, she faded out of their son's life.

Macoby and Mnookin (1992) observe that parents frequently raise concerns about the other parent's competence in legal disputes in order to build their legal argument. It can be very hard initially for a third party (a court, for instance, or a mediator) to clarify when that is not the case and one parent, in fact, is severely disturbed.

THE ROLE OF IMMATURE AND PSYCHOTIC DEFENSES IN PARTNERS' FAILURE TO DISENGAGE

An examination of marital partners' defenses against core feelings (shame, guilt, disappointment, sorrow) that are catalyzed by the breakup of a marriage helps to illuminate how conflict between former spouses can escalate and remain unresolved. From a developmental perspective, children and adolescents require adequate parenting to internalize sufficient internal mechanisms (what psychoanalysts refer to as ego strength) to process strong affects. Adults who lacked the earlier opportunity to master difficult affects implement defenses—either immature or psychotic, according to Vaillant's categories—that completely block access to underlying feelings. Severe early trauma, too, can result in the inability to process affects (Krystal, 1991).

Mr. Neal, severely under-parented as a child, struggled throughout adolescence and early adulthood with social isolation and pervasive feelings of inadequacy. He was astonished in his early thirties when a woman found him attractive and wanted to marry him. However, when his wife became fed up with his controlling, jealous mode of interacting and left after eight years, Mr. Neal became seriously depressed and then consumed with bitterness. He initiated a ferocious court battle for custody of his daughter, Chloe, which he eventually won.

After numerous court battles, Mr. Neal refused his ex-wife access to Chloe. He had convinced himself that she had a severe borderline personality disorder, a disorder he researched extensively and whose diagnostic criteria he memorized. (While she was emotionally vulnerable, there was no evidence ✱ Ms. Neal was so disturbed.) He hired a pugnacious attorney and a "hired gun" forensic psychologist to testify on his behalf. Controlled and articulate, Mr. Neal managed to convince the judge that his ex-wife posed a grave threat to Chloe. In contrast, as he presented it, he was essentially flawless. The passage of time had done nothing to ameliorate Mr. Neal's outrage. He could not talk about his ex-wife without spitting venom.

Mr. Neal adopted the immature defense of splitting whereby negative self-attributes such as hostility and envy are disavowed and attributed to another person. People who split defensively free themselves of ideas of badness and burdensome responsibility for negative behaviors by making the other person the repository for these experiences of the self. By attributing all disturbance to his wife and exaggerating his own virtues, Mr. Neal disowned a role in the demise of his marriage, protecting his fragile self-esteem. By viewing his wife as disturbed, he also could invalidate his reasons for having loved her (i.e., how could he possibly love someone so awful?), thus assuring himself there was no reason to feel sad about losing her. Fully defended against awareness of the hurt and sadness he did feel, Mr. Neal focused only on his righteous mission to protect his daughter from her "crazy" mother. That trajectory is common in the high-conflict divorce—acute anguish at the separation followed by the consolidation of a rigid defensive stance.

In one sense, immature and psychotic defenses such as splitting are successful because they allow people to distance themselves fully from intolerable feelings. In other ways, though, they are highly problematic because they:

- Interfere with mourning
- Contribute to interpersonal conflict
- Interfere with empathy
- Interfere with moral functioning
- Interfere with self-reflectiveness

How Immature and Psychotic Defenses Interfere with Mourning

The hallmark of high-conflict divorce is the suspended-in-time quality of ex-spouses' engagement, which derives, at least in part, from their inability to integrate underlying feelings sufficiently to mourn. Mr. Neal is not mourning. We see no awareness of sorrow or guilt, no rewriting of a "divorce script" that reflects increasing awareness of his role in the marital problems or empathy for his ex-wife's travails. The psychological imperative to keep sorrow and hurt out of conscious awareness takes precedence over—and renders impossible—a goodbye. Projective defenses—which place intolerable feelings outside oneself—invariably impede mourning because mourning, by definition, means working with them internally.

How Immature and Psychotic Defenses Contribute to Interpersonal Conflict

People who cannot tolerate loss tend to turn intrapsychic conflict (e.g., how can I bear the sorrow of saying goodbye to someone I love?) into interpersonal conflict. Whereas an adult whose gradual acceptance of loss leads to the conclusion, "what happened, happened," a Mr. Neal insists that what happened should not have happened: It was unfair, immoral or just plain wrong (Steiner, 2005). Such people, then, do not see their task post-divorce as mastering internal struggles over loss. They believe, instead, that they must fight to rectify injustice.

Those who project ugly qualities onto others contribute to interpersonal tensions additionally because when people are turned into a repository for others' projections, they often fight back, triggering the never-ending litany of accusations and counter-accusations that characterize high-conflict divorces.

> *Mr. Neal's wife, outraged by her ex-husband's assertion that she had a personality disorder, denied any psychological problems and countered that he was "paranoid," a view affirmed by her therapist, who was offended that her patient was under attack. Mr. Neal responded furiously that Ms. Neal's "outrageous accusation" confirmed his original diagnosis of borderline personality disorder.*

Johnston and Campbell (1988) suggest that some feuding spouses stay locked into dysfunctional relationships *because* they need the other spouse to stay available as a repository for projected aspects of themselves. Splitting creates a rigid, black-and-white (good-versus-bad) version of complex reality. Johnston and Campbell describe these individuals' cognitive styles:

> Under the prevailing distressed emotional states of the parties, thinking becomes more concrete, stylized, fragmented and not integrated with other as-

pects of their understanding. Perceptual narrowing and distortion occur, all of
which is conducive to stereotyped thinking, simplistic characterizations and
broad generalizations about the other (p. 65).

Dealing with individuals who defensively split leaves almost no room to
maneuver: One either aligns with their particular worldview or one is against
them. An adversarial legal system in which one person "wins" and the other
"loses" reinforces polarized positions, often contributing to escalation.

Other immature defenses contribute to interpersonal tensions. Hypochondriasis is framed by Vaillant (1977) as a persistent, angry accusation that
another person has been damaging; it is used to manage unacceptable feelings of aggression and locks the ostensibly damaged person into an accusato-
ry stance with the person who presumably caused the damage. Delusional
projection, a psychotic defense, also relies on others to serve as the repository of projections. Projected accusations can become reified over time: even
ten years post-divorce one spouse might be characterized as "crazy" and the
other as a "pathological narcissist."

Immature and psychotic defenses contribute to interpersonal conflict in
others ways. Because people overwhelmed by loss implement defenses with
ferocious urgency—like calling out the National Guard in response to an
emergency—they cling to them with desperate rigidity, terrified of unmanageable affects seeping through. They seek people around them to buttress
their defenses, often forcefully enjoining others to align with their defensive-
ly-wrought vision of the marriage and divorce. These people—new partners
as well as extended family and community members—are quickly drawn into
the conflict, the phenomenon that Johnston and Campbell (1988) describe as
"tribal warfare."

> Mr. Neal's harsh views of his wife were not open to discussion. He dismissed
> people who questioned him, even his few friends, as blindly ignorant or as
> colluding with the enemy. His absolute certainty and the threat of exclusion
> from his orbit of anyone who disagreed with him polarized his family of origin.
> Some allied with him against his ex-wife, agreeing she was "disturbed." Oth-
> ers, who had been fond of Ms. Neal during the marriage, dismissed Mr. Neal
> as irrational and cruel.

"Tribal warfare" is not simply one-directional. Because divorcing individuals
are vulnerable to the influence of others, especially around traumatic separations, family members, therapists and attorneys can inflame them, spurring
them to retributive action. People surrounding vulnerable parents have their
own motivations to battle. Extended family members often are driven by the
power of blood-ties and their need to consolidate a sense of us versus them as
they themselves struggle with deeply unsettling emotional reactions to the
divorce. Some lawyers, invested in litigation, see an opportunity for the kind

of courtroom brawl they relish. Therapists can have any number of their own, often unconscious, motivations to spur escalation of a conflict.

How Immature and Psychotic Defenses Interfere with Empathy

People who implement psychotic or immature defenses in response to loss are usually impervious to the needs and feelings of the people they rely upon to buttress their defenses because their primary goal in relationships is maintaining psychic equilibrium.

> *Ms. Oates considered her ex-husband a "callous son of a bitch." Hurt by his decision to end their brief marriage, she disparaged him constantly and tightly controlled access to their son, Dale. Dale adored his father, who was somewhat loutish but was deeply devoted to him, and grieved their lack of contact. Mr. Oates was heartbroken at his limited time with Dale. He could not comprehend why his ex-wife, though understandably angry that he left her, could not recognize that he was a loving father.*

Ms. Oates could not allow herself to be aware of Mr. Oates's strengths, Dale's love for his father, or their sorrow at their limited contact. To do so would have meant being in touch with qualities in her ex-husband that Ms. Oates herself had adored and could not bear to acknowledge since he left her.

How Immature and Psychotic Defenses Interfere with Moral Functioning

The aforementioned defensive need to disparage the ex-spouse was entirely justified in Ms. Oates's mind: He damaged her and must pay. When we turn another person into the repository of badness, we can justify almost any action we direct against them. Parents locked into bitter feuding rarely show apprehension of—or concern about—the terrible damage they are causing.

> *A man, outraged that his ex-wife refused to engage in an argument when she was picking up their son, tried to punch her through the window of her truck, shattering the window and showering her with glass as their son cowered in the back seat. He blamed her for driving away when he was trying to talk with her.*

Even violence can be justified.

How Immature and Psychotic Defenses Interfere with Self-Reflectiveness

Constructive mourning, as described, is a developmental process in which a person gradually comes to a richer understanding of reality. In the years following his divorce, a man might come to recognize that his temper was a genuine liability in his marriage and that his ex-wife had some justifiable concerns about his volatility. His ex-wife for her part might recognize that her unrealistically high expectations of men burden relationships unduly, or, alternatively, she might conclude that she has been too easily accepting of men's angry outbursts and needs to become more self-assertive. Divorcing partners who defensively need to blame the other person for the failure of the marriage and deny their own role are unable to develop their capacity for self-reflection, however.

> *Ms. Oates, interviewed by a court-appointed mediator, offered the following explanation for the post-divorce impasse: She is an excellent mother who continually tries hard and her ex-husband is a "creep" who makes no effort. In recounting their history, Ms. Oates explained that she was thwarted at every turn by her ex-husband's "bad character." When the mediator asked if there were things she might do differently to calm the feuding, Ms. Oates responded curtly, "no, there is nothing." She was offended that he would ask such a question because she had already explained that all problems emanated from her ex-husband's behavior.*

Such a lack of self-reflectiveness contributes to the frozen quality of high-conflict divorce because the feuding parties do not change. Many parents caught in high-conflict divorces, prone to externalization of their problems, do not seek mental health services (Johnston and Campbell, 1988).

Chapter Four

Breakdowns in Connection between Parents and Children around Divorce

SOME INTRINSIC CHALLENGES OF DIVORCE FOR CHILDREN

Even in the best of circumstances (e.g., where conflict is minimal), divorce presents challenges to children. Divorce by definition involves a drastic change in family structure, which involves the loss of the family unit and 1 disruption to routine. It often means a downward shift in financial status, 2 which strains family members. Over the course of years, divorce means 3 repeated goodbyes as children leave one parent's home to go to the other's as well as some (often considerable) time away from each parent. When children are attached to both parents, every separation is, at the least, somewhat 4 stressful and, at the most, overwhelmingly painful. (The child's age, quality of attachment to both parents, and the specifics of the parenting arrangement bear heavily on the impact of separations.)

After a separation and divorce, even when conflict is low, children have to negotiate two universes, each with its own value systems and rhythms. Where parents were once responsible for trying to reconcile differences between themselves, children must reconcile those differences after parents split, and that is an often lonely, confusing task (Marquardt, 2005). Children often face different rules and moral codes in two households, which can be bewildering and burdensome. Marquardt describes such experiences as being caught "between two worlds." Research confirms her findings (Finley and Schwartz, 2010). When their parents are at odds, children face loyalty conflicts: If I enjoy being with one parent am I neglecting the other? Children's loyalty conflicts are accentuated when parents begin dating: If I like my mother's/father's new boyfriend/girlfriend, am I being disloyal?

In two-parent households that run well, parents coordinate household logistics. They make sure the children get where they need to go (activities, doctor's appointments) and have what they need (lunch money, sports equipment). Parents face daily decisions about their children, some large and some small: Is a daycare provider adequate or understaffed? Is a neighborhood boy a bully to be avoided? Is it okay to miss church group in order to go to dance practice? Is the child playing too many video games? In well-functioning household environments, parents work together to find reasonable resolutions to such questions. But, when parents set out to create new lives apart from each other, coordination between parents diminishes. Macoby and Mnookin (1992) found a considerable decline in the frequency with which parents spoke to each other over three and a half years following parental separation. Avoidance of communication increases with the passage of time and contributes to many children's sense that they are living in two worlds that hardly overlap.

Children tend to assume that parents are supposed to sacrifice on their behalf, yet divorcing parents privilege their own needs over their children's (with possible exceptions, such as domestic violence and mental illness). No matter how much children assume personal responsibility for their parents' divorce, divorce exposes them to the reality that their parents have made decisions that do not take them into account and also to their parents' emotional vulnerabilities, including their failure to work out differences in their marriage. In the face of parents' emotional upset, children often experience helplessness because they cannot intervene. On a practical level, children of divorce have to negotiate such logistical challenges as bringing school supplies back and forth as they work to create a viable life in two households. Demands for high levels of organization burden all children and overwhelm some (e.g., children with ADHD).

A CHILD-CENTERED APPROACH TO DIVORCE

Given these myriad challenges for children, there are ways divorcing parents can work together and with their children to reduce children's suffering.

Reaching Agreements Pre-Divorce

Ideally, divorcing parents would figure out together what their post-separation parenting arrangement would look like before speaking to their children about the divorce. A planned unfolding of events would avoid chaotic scenes likely to stress or even traumatize their children. For infants and toddlers, parents would be especially attuned to the risk of extended separations from the primary caregiver (assuming there is one) and the need for a consistent, structured parenting arrangement that creates predictability. For school-age children, they would create a parenting arrangement that would enhance the child's ability to manage school and recreational activities and accommodate the child's growing investment in the world of peers.

If parents were at odds about the parenting arrangement, they would agree not to litigate their differences, understanding that litigation takes critical parenting decisions out of their hands. Instead, they would consult a mental health professional with expertise in divorce to help them. The parents would agree to meet with that expert periodically if tensions arise and to fine-tune their parenting arrangement to take heed of changes in the family and the children's evolving developmental needs.

Parents, recognizing that arguing stresses children, would agree not to argue in front of them. Also, recognizing that children need to feel as comfortable as possible living in two homes, they would agree to speak respectfully of each other and respect and reinforce each other's discipline. Parents, aware that children feel burdened when they have to coordinate households and find it reassuring when parents come together to manage their care, would agree to stay in close contact with each other and, ideally, would establish specific plans for being in touch.

Talking to the Children About the Divorce

Once they arrived at clarity, parents would sit down with the children together and explain in age-appropriate terms that the parents are going to be living apart and explain in detail what the parenting arrangement will look like. (With older children, parents would integrate the children's wishes into their planning.) The parents would talk about how sad this event is and offer the children a space to discuss their sadness and anxiety. Without breaking down and burdening the children with their own suffering, the parents might speak about their own sadness as a way of encouraging the children to express theirs. While acknowledging the hard parts of the pending divorce, the parents would reassure the children that they will remain loved and attended to by both parents. The parents would address whatever concerns the children had, acknowledging that children have different worries at different points along the way and affirming that the parents will want to know about them.

Co-Parenting Constructively Post-Divorce

Once the parents split, they would track how the children were faring—in terms of mood, for instance, and peer relations. When one parent observed changes, that parent would touch base with the other to see what he or she was observing and consider interventions. They would anticipate that child-rearing challenges, even crises, would inevitably arise. They would proceed respectfully and cautiously with each other at such stressful times and seek help if they found themselves at odds. Parents would reach out regularly to their children, noting aloud that the parent is aware the child is dealing with stresses of a new family situation and wondering how the child is managing. If the child pushes the parent away, the parent would understand that the child is probably denying upsetting feelings and would persist in finding ways, perhaps in consultation with an expert, to help the child open up so the parent and child did not drift apart. Parents would express genuine interest in how life is going for the child at the other parent's house without conveying intrusive curiosity or hostility.

Parents might place a child in therapy if they were concerned about the child's mental health. However, they would be actively involved in the therapy themselves in order to stay tuned in to their child's distress. Parents would monitor themselves carefully to ensure that their emotional upheaval in response to the divorce did not interfere with their parenting (e.g., by their relying on their children for comfort). They would attend carefully to their own moods and intake of alcohol (and other substances). They would exercise regularly and mobilize support systems. If they found themselves depressed or withdrawn, they would seek help from a therapist. When the parents begin to date, they would be conservative about introducing the children to new lovers. They would be appropriately cautious about such inflammatory matters as involving a new partner in the child's discipline.

Dealing with Children's Special Needs

Children with medical or psychiatric difficulties present challenges to all parents. For instance, how do parents ascertain if a school-age child with academic difficulties has ADHD? What if the diagnosis falls in a gray area? Should one seek stimulant medication? What about behavioral expectations for a child with Asperger's Syndrome or the best medication for a child with severe rheumatoid arthritis? Does a child have a serious depression or is she or he just blue? When parents are working to disengage from each other, the urgent need to coalesce to address such challenges can be extremely difficult. Optimally, divorcing parents whose children face such challenges would create a forum for addressing ongoing issues in consultation with an agreed-upon expert (e.g., psychologist, psychiatrist, pediatrician, social worker).

Clinicians who deal with divorce are likely to find this characterization sadly far removed from situations they see in their offices. We can ask why many parents, even those who are genuinely devoted to their children, have such difficulty implementing a child-centered approach to separation and divorce? Parents' capacity for empathy is contingent upon a number of factors, including affect tolerance, capacity for intimacy, and their own experiences of parental empathy (or lack thereof) in growing up. In addition, parents' emotional responses to separation and loss influence their sensitivity to their children. Even highly empathic parents tend to manifest circumscribed lapses in empathy for their children following a divorce. In their ten-year follow-up of divorced parents, Wallerstein, Lewis, and Blakeslee (2000) found that only half of the mothers and a quarter of the fathers were able to provide the same level of nurturant care that distinguished their parenting prior to the divorce. Parents who have always had difficulties with empathy usually show more egregious lapses post-divorce. Much of the difficulty lies in the intersection between parents' and children's emotional responses to divorce.

CHILDREN'S DEFENSES AGAINST MOURNING

Like grown-ups, children must mourn the losses in divorce in order to move on with their lives and invest energetically in new relationships and activities. Children's mourning, like that of adults, includes confronting and coming to terms with painful realities. It is hard, though, for children to stay aware of these realities without blaming themselves or lapsing into denial. Like grown-ups, too, children in mourning must manage and modulate their grief, and, again like grown-ups but even more so, children have trouble bearing painful feelings. Unless a trusted person can empathically resonate with them and communicate that their feelings of sadness, hurt, and anger are understandable, reasonable reactions to difficult circumstances, children tend to feel guilty and ashamed, as though they were overreacting and creating difficulties where they need not exist.

Many children of divorce, acutely attuned to their parents' suffering, fear that their anger and disappointment will further burden their parents. They are prone then to block out awareness of their true feelings about divorce through defensive maneuvers particular to their developmental stages (Kalter, 1990). Preschoolers tend to displace anger at their parents onto others, expressing fury at a classmate or teacher, for instance. Elementary school children implement a range of defensive maneuvers to obscure their emotional distress, according to Kalter: somatic complaints, emotional detachment, social withdrawal, intellectualizing, displacing feelings. Girls are more prone to reaction formation or intellectualization. Boys are more inclined to act out aggressively.

Children's angry reactions to divorce function as adults' do to block out awareness of sadness and hurt. Increased aggression in children and adolescents can also reflect an identification with parental violence and aggression (Wallerstein and Kelly, 1980): Being *like* the angry parent covers over underlying helplessness and anxiety in the face of parents' explosive behaviors (the defense of identification with the aggressor). Similarly, identification with absent parents—often the father—seeks to undo the reality of loss (Kalter, 1990; Tessman, 1996): By becoming *like* the absent parent, the child denies the parent's absence.

✳   Children, through their defensive responses to disruption and loss, seek to "solve" pressing inner struggles: How can I deal with being so sad? How can I be so mad at my mom and my dad? How can it be okay for me to feel so disappointed in my parents when they themselves are so torn up about the end of the marriage? Children, by keeping parents at arms' length, can distance themselves from loving feelings that have come to feel conflicted in the face of their disappointment. But children's defenses, like those of adults, also *create* difficulties: Children lose track of their own underlying distress so they cannot ask for help with what really ails them. A preschool boy who hits a classmate cannot let his parents know how angry he is at them for divorcing because he himself does not know. A school-age girl who expresses sadness through frequent stomachaches cannot ask grown-ups for help with her sorrow because she does not recognize it as such.

In addition, children, unable to stay in touch with underlying hurt and sadness, become self-critical in response to "bad behavior" and lose empathy for themselves. Wallerstein (1989), in her follow-up study of children of divorce, was struck by how cut off from their feelings and memories many young adults were. Since childhood, they had put enormous psychic energy into denying their anguish about their parents' divorce. Put differently, they had been unable to bear difficult feelings sufficiently to mourn the losses. For some, a failure to mourn interfered with their capacities to invest emotional energy in new endeavors, especially intimate relationships.

SOME FACTORS THAT LEAD PARENTS AND CHILDREN TO DRIFT APART AROUND DIVORCE

Lack of Preparation for the Pending Separation

Children find divorce easiest to comprehend after years of overt marital conflict, but they often are surprised by their parents' announcement of divorce because they had no idea trouble was brewing and parents did not think to warn them. In one study, a third of children in divorcing households were only briefly aware of their parents' unhappiness prior to their parents' decision to divorce (Wallerstein and Kelly, 1980). Many children are told about a pending divorce in a cursory manner (Dunn et al., 2001). Eighty percent of children are not provided with an adequate explanation of the divorce with assurance of continued care (Wallerstein, 1989). Many parents, absorbed in a catastrophic rupture, lack the presence of mind to sit down with their children and calmly explain what is going on and what changes are pending, and then to attend carefully to their children's concerns. Babies and toddlers are most vulnerable to the outpouring of emotion and sudden changes in the care-giving environment (Kalter, 1990).

Adults' Difficulties Understanding Children's Defenses

Adults, including teachers and parents, by focusing on children's outward behaviors, often lose sight of the emotional suffering that propels children's defensiveness.

> *Martha, twelve, hurt by her parents' divorce, especially her father's move to a distant city, withdrew to her room where she listened to dark music and experimented with heavy black make-up. Her mother asked her a few times if she was okay and Martha responded curtly, "I'm fine." Exasperated and feeling cut off, her mother finally blew up, angrily criticizing Martha for withdrawing from the family and being "morbid."*

> *Alex, ten, was deeply hurt that his mother was so absorbed in work and a new boyfriend in the months that followed the divorce that she stopped coming to his soccer games. But, aware of her high stress level and worried he was being selfish, he did not say anything. Instead, Alex, once a model student, began acting out in school. His parents and teachers rebuked him for behaving badly. No one asked if he were hurting.*

Children's hostile behaviors burden parents and create considerable disruption in many divorce situations. The convergence of increased aggressive behaviors in children in response to divorce and weary parents (often mothers) too worn out to set adequate limits is one of the gravest problems in some post-divorce families. However, children's problem behaviors can divert attention from a more troubling reality: The child is suffering. Divorcing parents often are more disposed to confront a child's "bad behavior" than confront (and bear) a child's sorrow.

PARENTS' DIFFICULTIES IN INITIATING MEANINGFUL CONVERSATION WITH THEIR CHILDREN

It is commonplace for parents, at the behest of experts, to tell their children that the divorce is "not your fault." Such a comment is one of two things (the other being assurance of their unwavering love) that many parents say to support their children around a divorce. Such reassurance is useful as far as it goes because children, indeed, can feel burdened by a sense of guilty responsibility, but the intervention fails to address a more troubling reality: In most instances, parents' decision to divorce has *nothing* to do with their children. Given the choice between feeling responsible and recognizing the awful reality that parents are acting without them in mind, children are inclined to insist that the parents' difficulties have *something* to do with them. For preschoolers, the burdensome sense of responsibility emanates in cognitive egocentrism; as children grown older, they often cling defensively to an egocentric stance to stave off feelings of helplessness. In other words, children hold tight to the notion that if the divorce had something to do with them (e.g., they were too angry), then potentially they can influence their parents' to reverse course (e.g., by being more amicable). Parents' reassurance, then, about the child's having no responsibility fails to address the core underlying experience of helplessness.

Parents (along with teachers, pediatricians and others) have little or no training in talking to children about their inner lives and come to interactions with their children with unrealistic expectations, including the idea that children will welcome the opportunity to share their emotional distress (Kalter, 1990). Kalter notes, too, that children have a very hard time putting their feelings into words, lacking the cognitive-affective integration necessary to find language for difficult feelings. Many parents, even when they sense their children are hurting, have difficulty knowing what to say that will promote meaningful dialogue. Instead they approach their children with direct, often general questions. When children and adolescents are defensively downplaying emotional upset, parents' direct confrontation of those feelings bypasses their defenses, making them acutely uncomfortable. Children, then, are prone to push parents away by responding briefly in a manner that communicates unwillingness to engage.

Many divorcing parents feel as though they have failed as parents due to their inability to protect their children from the fallout of divorce. When their children shut them down with monosyllabic answers, they feel even more inadequate. Having borne rejection and hurt in relation to the spouse, many cannot bear rejection from their children and are disposed to withdraw self-protectively. They might rationalize their withdrawal by thinking, for instance, "my child needs some space" or "I do not want to be intrusive." A negative feedback loop can occur: Children, feeling hurt by the divorce, push parents away; parents, feeling hurt and inadequate, withdraw further; children, hurt and confused by that withdrawal, fend off their parents even more assiduously; and so on. Over time, many children and parents in divorce situations give up on having meaningful contact. Only *one third* of young adults who grew up in divorced households went to their parents for comfort, as opposed to two thirds of young adults from intact families (Marquardt, 2005).

Some divorcing parents contact child therapists because they feel discouraged about making meaningful contact with their children. They have tried unsuccessfully to broach the topic of the divorce and feel stuck. Parents are then left offering the child platitudes that they themselves know have little effect in breaking down walls. Feeling worried and worn down, they place the child in therapy in the hope that at least someone will be able to connect with their child emotionally. Empathetic child therapists, indeed, can help children in divorce situations a great deal, but some child therapists, because of their absorption in individual work and, perhaps, because they feel confused about how to help stuck parents, fail to provide parents with the assistance they need to reestablish meaningful connections with their children. Children for their part, while they appreciate the empathy of a kind therapist, can feel that their parents are shunting them off to another person's care and feel even more pessimistic about their parents understanding what they are going through.

Part of the difficulty is that is can be hard, indeed, to find a way to speak with children who are strenuously denying their suffering. Parents have to be persistent and patient and understand something about how children's defenses work. Hagman (1995a) points out that bereaved people (in this context children) are "exquisitely sensitive" to failures in empathy (p. 203). When parents (cursorily) ask children if everything is okay, and do not follow up when the child responds (cursorily) that, yes, everything is okay, children understand that parents really mean: I *need* everything to be okay. Children tend to be much more attuned to their parents' emotional conflicts than parents recognize, and they discern when a parent is unable to tolerate their sorrow about the divorce.

> *Tony, a sensitive, self-reflective twelve-year-old, felt devastated when his father quickly remarried after the divorce and threw himself into the relationship with his new wife to the exclusion of his time with Tony. When Tony tried to bring his distress to his father's attention, his father resonated with it briefly but then told his son it was time to move on. He used his remarriage to provide what he saw as a teachable moment, telling his son: "Life is about dealing with challenges."*

Tony felt furious that his father was lecturing him about managing his life, as opposed to recognizing how deeply he had hurt him. He withdrew into stony silence.

Many divorced parents tell child therapists that their children have not mentioned having any problems; parents seize onto that fact as hoped-for evidence that the child is unencumbered by the divorce. When therapists inquire carefully, however, they usually find that children have provided parents with subtle—and not so subtle—indications that the divorce is very much on their minds.

> *Dr. Parekh, two years post-divorce, mentioned to her therapist that her teenage daughters seemed to be managing the aftermath of the divorce extremely well. She mentioned almost in passing, though, that both girls had made brief remarks about Dr. Parekh's new boyfriend and their sense that he might not*

be such a good stepfather. They also spoke about a friend whose mother's remarriage was a disaster.

In order for parents to connect in a meaningful way with their child's inner experience of the divorce, parents must be able to see through a child's defenses so they can appreciate the child's underlying distress, persist in reaching out to the child even after being rebuffed, and be genuinely open to hearing about the child's true feelings.

PARENTS' FAILURE TO ADDRESS CHILDREN'S DISAPPOINTMENT IN THEIR DIVORCING PARENTS

Bearing and integrating their disappointment in their parents for divorcing is a critical feature of mourning post-divorce, but children cannot manage it without help. Children fear, usually justifiably, that they will hurt their parents' feelings and provoke a backlash if they express their disappointment directly. Indeed, it is extremely difficult for most parents to let in awareness of their children's disappointment, even when it is warranted, because they already feel guilty about the divorce. When children express these feelings ("you and mom/dad messed up my life by splitting up"), parents are prone to reflexively rebuke them for being disrespectful or hostile; they find it hard to parlay children's disappointment and anger into meaningful dialogue, contributing to a growing gulf between them and their children.

PARENTS' ABSORPTION IN MOURNING AND ITS IMPACT ON CHILDREN

The greatest barrier to parents connecting with their children's inner experience of divorce often lies in *the intersection between parents' mourning and children's emotional reactions to divorce* because the very process of mourning in which parents are engaged tends to preclude the empathic attunement that children so urgently need.

> *Ms. Quinn, an accomplished consultant and attentive mother was overcome with hurt and fury after her husband announced he was gay and was leaving her and moved into an apartment nearby. The couple agrees to consult with a psychologist to help them deal thoughtfully with their six-year-old daughter. Ms. Quinn affixes the psychologist with an unwavering glare and wonders what the point is of talking with her daughter about the family situation.*
>
> *The therapist suggests that the little girl, who has been especially clingy, must be feeling confused and sad and would feel less isolated if her mother spoke with her about the separation and pending divorce. Ms. Quinn responds tersely that her daughter already knows that the separation "sucks," and that*

talking about it will only reinforce how bad it really is. In addition, she says, talking will not undo what has happened because the damage is done.

After a few more futile attempts to help Ms. Quinn intervene with her daughter, the therapist realizes that nothing but undoing the terrible reality of her husband's leaving would matter for her at this moment. Ms. Quinn, hurt and furious and struggling to integrate an intolerable turn of events, can only imagine that her daughter wants exactly what she herself longs for—a reversal of that experience. Because she cannot provide that for her daughter, she feels she cannot provide anything useful and, therefore, cannot appreciate that speaking to the changes in the family would help her daughter.

The therapist also realizes that Ms. Quinn is unable to take in his suggestions because he cannot undo the reality of her husband's betrayal. On her return for additional sessions several months later, however, Ms. Quinn is much more receptive to the therapist's ideas about how to address her daughter's experience. Having begun to come to terms with her husband's departure, she has become more amenable to thinking about what her daughter is going through.

Many divorcing parents are ambivalent about *really knowing* what their child is experiencing emotionally even when, consciously, they believe they want to know because children's grief about the divorce resonates with parents' grief and parents cannot bear their children's sorrow when they cannot bear their own.

> *Mr. Reed struggled to move on with his life after his wife indicated she wanted a divorce. A devoted father, deeply concerned about his sons, eight and ten, he tried a few times to talk to them about the divorce. When they were taciturn, he gave up. Mr. Reed's therapist confronted him with what appeared to be minimal effort for a man who was usually determined. Mr. Reed agreed that his efforts were minimal and, upon reflection, said he could not stand the idea that his boys would tell him they were as brokenhearted as he was.*

Such halfhearted attempts at connecting with a child's underlying feelings is highly unlikely to succeed.

For many parents, children represent the culmination of marital intimacy, including sexual intimacy. Just dealing with the children after a divorce, then, catalyzes painful feelings because children have become a stark reminder of what has been lost. To avoid these feelings, divorcing parents are vulnerable to withdrawing from their children, often without conscious awareness they are doing so.

> *Dr. Stein treasured the time at home during his marriage when the family could be together. He and his wife, though often distant, took pleasure in raising their four children. They took frequent family excursions on weekends*

and enjoyed vacations in Mexico. After the divorce, Dr. Stein often found himself full of sorrow when he spent time with his children. Though he enjoyed their company, he could not help remembering close times they had spent together as a family. He found school events and sporting events especially hard, as his ex-wife sat in a different section of the auditorium or gym. Dr. Stein could not even consider speaking to his children about his—and their— sorrow because he feared he would cry, burdening them unduly.

Baum (2004) offers the prescient insight that some fathers withdraw from their children post-divorce because they view their children and ex-wife as a single entity as a consequence of their failure to come to terms with the end of the marital relationship. Only when they are helped to mourn the end of their marriage can they re-engage their children more energetically.

CHILDREN'S ALONENESS FOLLOWING DIVORCE

Elizabeth Marquardt (2005) provides a moving firsthand account of growing up with divorced parents. She suggests that much of the burden children face, even when there is minimal parental conflict, concerns children's isolation because grown-ups fail to acknowledge children's experiences of loss. She writes: "If there is any single experience that unites children of divorce it is our feelings of loneliness as children" (p. 48). She elaborates: "Some of us felt lonely not only because we were often alone but also because we were isolated by intense and unacknowledged emotions" (p. 49). As an example, when she was seven years old, she heard a mother on the playground describe children of divorce as being like footballs that are kicked back and forth between their parents. When she shared the image with her father, he became agitated and appeared angry. As Marquardt recalls, her father did not ask how *she* felt going back and forth between two households or what about the image of the football captured her imagination. Instead, he told her sternly that the image did not apply to her because both parents loved her. His apparent need to frame the divorce in positive terms impeded his ability to recognize his daughter's effort to communicate something about *her* experience.

 Marquardt says that the "between-two-worlds" experience of children of divorce is especially confusing and rarely acknowledged. She recalls an instance when, at her father's home, she used the phrase "screwed up" that she used at her mother's home. Her father corrected her firmly, saying "messed up." Marquardt recalls feeling silly and ashamed. Her father, apparently, was unaware of her bind—caught between households with different rules. In this interaction, the girl's father, who is described as a decent, loving man, missed the chance to connect meaningfully with his daughter's experience of the divorce and its aftermath. He might have said, *"You know, I prefer that*

you don't use the language 'screwed up' when you are in my house. I prefer ✽✽
'messed up.' But I can imagine that is confusing for you, given that your
mother and I have different ideas about appropriate language." By failing to
appreciate and respond sensitively to his daughter's divorce-created bind, the
father contributed to her sense of shame at *her* putative failure.

Family systems theory posits that the larger family system holds family
members together, causing their behaviors to be interrelated (Finley and
Schwartz, 2010). Divorce creates multiple family systems in which children
are the only common link. Divorced parents can either mitigate children's ΣITH
experience of separate worlds by coordinating care and creating a relatively ╱
coherent caregiving environment or accentuate it by being hostile or indiffer- OR
ent.

Wallerstein (1989), also citing the centrality of children's loneliness,
found that *fewer than 10 percent of children had an adult speak to them
sympathetically about their parents' divorce.* That lack of meaningful conversation leaves children feeling they have to manage the myriad challenges
of divorce on their own. Twice as many young adults from divorced households as young adults who grew up with both parents agreed strongly with
the statement, "I always felt like an adult, even when I was a little kid"
(Marquardt, 2005, p. 53). Even divorces that eventually settle down may
have eruptions of rage and even violence. Children have no way to understand their parents' alarming behaviors as a response to divorce. No way, that
is, unless they are provided with the kind of detailed, sensitive feedback
children rarely receive.

SOME CHALLENGES FOR NON-CUSTODIAL PARENTS

Many parents fail to grasp the impact on children of fathers living outside the
household, assuming, incorrectly, that regular visits feel about the same to
children as daily contact, even if that contact was minimal pre-divorce (Kalter, 1990). Non-custodial parents often feel relegated to the periphery of their
children's lives and increasingly inadequate to the challenges of parenting.
Less involved, non-custodial parents tend to become less aware of their
children's evolving developmental needs. Non-custodial fathers are the most
lenient of parents (Hetherington and Kelly, 2002); their role tends to be
"companionate rather than parental" (p. 119). Structured "visits" with a parent can feel strained; children often have trouble with transitions and might
be hesitant about leaving their primary caregiver to stay in an apartment or
house that feels strange to them.

In a defensive effort to manage feeling inadequate in relation to their
children, some non-custodial fathers pull back from engaging in their children's lives. Conflicts with an ex-wife and feeling a lack of control over

decisions regarding their children also lead some fathers to withdraw (Hetherington and Kelly, 2002). Some fail to comprehend the profound impact of their withdrawal on their children. Numerous authors (e.g., Warshak, 1992; Finley and Schwartz, 2010) have argued that it does not serve children's best interests to establish custodial arrangements that place fathers in a marginal role.

SOME CHALLENGES OF NEW PARTNERS

New partners offer the possibility of enrichment for children when an adult forms a positive relationship with a child over time; however, new partners also can be a source of tension and unhappiness. The outcome depends in significant part on how parents manage the situation. Children tend to see new partners as competitors for a parent's time and affection, an especially pressing matter when a parent has already been less available in the difficult months following a divorce. New partners are painful reminders of the demise of their parents' relationship and, in children's minds, close the door on reconciliation. Also, when children begin to feel attached to a parent's new partner, they can feel they are being disloyal to the other parent. Furthermore children, still reeling from the divorce, may be wary of the chance of another loss; that wariness amplifies their hesitancy to attach, which may run counter to the parent's wishes for the child to build a strong bond with the new partner. Hetherington and Kelly (2002) found that the remarriage of a former spouse often sparked in parents the re-emergence of feelings of loss, hurt, and anger that surrounded the divorce. These parents, then, especially mothers, were prone to accuse their children of disloyalty if they attached to a new partner.

Propelled by a wish to get beyond the pain of the marital breakup, some parents throw themselves into new relationships without adequately appreciating the impact of these relationships on their children. Overeagerness on the part of women is often stimulated by exhaustion and, for men, by a wish to rebuild a traditional paternal role (Hetherington and Kelly, 2002). Overeager parents can get caught up in the "myth of instant love" (Hodges, 1991, p. 224).

> *Ms. Tanner was delighted to find a new partner just six months after her divorce and was especially pleased with the idea that the man, a former marine, would help her manage her unruly sons, ages eight and thirteen. Quickly, however, her sons and new partner were arguing incessantly. The boys insisted furiously that they were unwilling to "take orders" from a man who was not their father. The man responded by becoming even more strict in his limit-setting, declaring that no child was going to talk back to him.*

Ms. Tanner, absorbed in her needs to consolidate a new relationship, attempted to confer a legitimacy upon her new partner for which her sons were unready. Some parents, eager to move on with their lives, introduce their children to new lovers before the parent has established that the relationship is serious, thus potentially exposing children to serial relationships. The presence of a new person in the parent's bedroom also exposes children to their parents' sexuality in a way that many children find uncomfortable and confusing.

PARENTIFIED CHILDREN

Where children in intact, loving marriages can represent the culmination of the parents' loving relationship, these meanings are destroyed by divorce. Some divorced parents, struggling to maintain their self-esteem, desperately lonely, revise their relationships with their children, turning to them to bolster that self-esteem and to function as confidantes. The nature and consequences of parents' misuse of their children generally corresponds to the child's age. A mother may cling physically to a preschooler, interfering with the child's developmental needs for gradual separation (Kalter, 1990). Grade-school children often are used for emotional support (Johnston and Campbell, 1988), and are expected to take on household tasks that ordinarily are parents' responsibility (Hodges, 1991).

Close relationships between mothers and daughters makes girls more likely to be a source of comfort and advice for their mothers (Hetherington and Kelly, 2002). Girls' inclination to take responsibility for their mothers' well-being can affect their efforts to establish more autonomy (Wallerstein, 1989). A father may parentify a preadolescent girl, placing her in a maternal or girlfriend-like role that stimulates anxiety-provoking oedipal longings in the youngster. In college-age adolescents whose parents divorced in their youth, there often is powerful evidence of distorted developmental trajectories as outgrowths of children's having attended to their parents' emotional needs during their childhoods. Their emotional vulnerabilities emerge forcefully when they strive to create viable, enriching lives apart from their parents.

Chapter Five

Entanglement with the Ex-Spouse

Its Impact on Children

Most divorced parents maintain good intentions about supporting their children's relationship with the other parent because they understand that children benefit from good relationships with both parents. However, despite this understanding, following through is not so easy. Because divorced parents, to varying degrees, remain emotionally bound up with their ex-spouses while they progress through a mourning process, their upsetting feelings about them influence their experience of—and responses to—their children's relationship with the other parent, often unconsciously. The more caught up in negative feelings from the marriage and divorce a parent is, the harder it will be for him or her to attend thoughtfully to a child's feelings about the other parent. This dynamic is most apparent in the high-conflict divorce but is evident in more subtle ways in most divorces.

PARENTS' DIFFICULTIES VALUING THE EX-SPOUSES' RELATIONSHIP WITH THE CHILDREN

One common obstacle derives from parents' tendency to distance themselves from awareness of ex-spouses' good qualities because being in touch with positive features of the ex-spouse stirs painful longings, especially in the first few years following divorce. Thus, divorced parents often have trouble taking pleasure in their children's joy at pleasurable experiences they had at the other home. Children pick up that their mothers do not want to hear about such experiences at their fathers' homes and vice versa. Because many children of divorce struggle to feel it is okay to love both parents, they look to each parent to approve their love for the other. When they pick up a parent's hesitancy or ambivalence, they may feel they have to favor one parent.

Staying aware of a child's strong connection to the other parent is hard for a parent who needs to deny his or her own longings for that parent.

> *Ms. Underwood, the primary caregiver of a son, six, and daughter, eight, complained that her ex-husband would not allow the children to call her during his week-long summer vacation in another state. Mr. Underwood countered that he had little enough time with the children as it was. He was not going to disrupt his precious vacation time so they could "gab" with their mother. Anyway, he said, her complaint was more about her failure to respect his autonomy as a father than the children's needs.*

The therapist found that both children were strained by their father's unwillingness to let them call their mother, with whom they were accustomed to having daily contact. She tried to discuss this with Mr. Underwood, but—caught up in a defensive need to disparage his ex-wife as a way to manage his sorrow over losing her—he could not be aware of how they missed their mother. Over time, unless Mr. Underwood can accept the loss of his marriage and move beyond his disguised longings for his ex-wife, he will not be able to appreciate the strength of his ex-wife's bond with the children and empathize with their experience of separations. They will feel they must hide their needs for their mother, even though expressing them is an extremely important part of their post-divorce experience. As a result, they will feel increasingly cut off from their father.

Supporting a child's relationship with the other parent is especially difficult when a marriage ends with a jarring rejection.

> *Mr. Vincente was bereft when his wife of fifteen years fell in love with a colleague at work and sought a divorce. When a therapist advised him to speak with his daughter, Portia, seven, about her parents' decision to live apart, Mr. Vincente stubbornly responded that he was unwilling to do so because the parents did not decide to live apart; his wife decided to leave him. For her part, Ms. Vincente insisted that divorce was inevitable because Mr. Vincente was unable to manage his life adequately.*

Mr. Vincente understood that Portia loved her mother and wanted to support their relationship. However, he was unable to put his feelings of grief and anger aside, at least at this time, so that he could speak to his daughter about the divorce in a way that did not paint her mother in a negative light (i.e., as the one to blame for ending the marriage).

Laura Heims Tessman (1996), a child psychoanalyst who has written extensively on parent loss, suggests that divorced parents, in interacting with their children, should not hide their anger or disappointment in the ex-spouse or deny the ex-spouse's realistic limitations when the child needs to recognize these. These are complex matters. Clearly, as Tessman argues, when a parent has abandoned a child, it is important for the remaining parent to help the child deal with that reality to diminish the impulse to self-blame and so the child can begin to mourn. Or, if a parent has committed a serious transgression such as violence, the other parent needs to help the child understand why such behavior is unacceptable. Even when a parent has abandoned a child or been violent, though, the remaining parent needs to be respectful of the *range* of feelings—longing, sorrow, love, rage—a child has toward that parent and not simply dismiss or disparage the parent out of anger or disappointment.

On the other hand, because divorcing parents are rarely neutral, their explanations of "reality" inevitably reflect their own ideas about the marriage and divorce. If Mr. Vincente angrily tells Portia that the marriage is ending because Portia's mother found another man and is leaving him—a version of reality—he runs the risk of driving a wedge between Portia and her mother. And, at least as Ms. Vincente would argue, the divorce is more complicated than that. At core, we can see that Mr. Vincente, understandably upset, faces a formidable challenge in establishing enough emotional distance from his wife to speak openly with Portia but not malign her mother (*"For many reasons, your mother and I can no longer live together. We both feel very hurt and angry and cannot seem to agree on anything, even why the marriage is not working out. It just doesn't make sense to stay together if we are always arguing. It's really sad and frustrating."*) Faced with such binds, many parents choose to avoid conversations about divorce altogether, leading children to feel the topic is out of bounds.

PARENTS' DIFFICULTIES SORTING OUT CHILDREN'S VIEWS FROM THE EX-SPOUSES'

Divorced parents' unresolved feelings about the ex-spouse can influence their interactions with their children in other harmful ways.

Sam's father viewed Sam's mother as overly protective of Sam, even coercive. When Sam, nine, told his father that he joined the computer club instead of the baseball team, Sam's father, a supporter of athletics, remarked dismissively, "there she goes again," implying that Sam made this choice because of his mother's influence. Sam felt hurt that his father could not see that he genuinely wanted to join the computer club. Mired in bitterness, Sam's father was unaware that his enmity toward Sam's mother obstructed an accurate perception of Sam's proclivities. He recalled feeling that his ex-wife tried to control him and assumed she was doing the same thing with Sam.

As is usually the case in families, this situation turned out to be complicated because Sam's father was partly right: Sam's mother, indeed, was overbearing. However, Sam's father could not talk with Sam's mother about Sam without an argument, and he could not discuss the matter with Sam without becoming angry. Over time, Sam became hesitant to speak with his father about his activities because he worried that his father would launch into a resentful critique of his mother. A vital piece of the father/son relationship was lost.

PARENTS' DIFFICULTIES ADDRESSING CHILDREN'S CHALLENGES IN NAVIGATING SEPARATE WORLDS

Secrets are common for children who travel back and forth between two households—not necessarily because parents insist on them but because children pick up accurately that parents do not want to hear about certain aspects of the child's life (Marquardt, 2005), such as the child's missing the other parent. Marquardt posits that children cannot help but feel that if a parent is not interested in what goes on in the other parent's home—a huge part of the child's life—then the parent is not that interested in the *child*. Unfortunately, a parent who is trying to detach emotionally from a former spouse is unlikely to express the sort of positive curiosity and interest in the other household that the child yearns for and that would knit the two households together. In addition, many divorced parents are not inclined to coalesce to coordinate care in a manner that would diminish the child's experience of navigating separate worlds, and their disagreements exacerbate that experience.

> *Robert, thirteen, was devoted to Boy Scouts and hoped to become an Eagle Scout. His father, unemployed, devoted many hours to being a scout leader. Robert's mother increasingly came to oppose the Boy Scouts because, she said, she was troubled by their views on homosexuality. She refused to finance Robert's scout trips; Robert's father was unable to do so. He pleaded with his ex-wife to help out, but she refused. He believed, correctly, that her antipathy toward the Boy Scouts was fueled in part by her anger at him.*

Parents caught in these sorts of conflicts, understandably, wish to share their vantage point on the conflict with their children. Robert's mother explained to her son that she was taking a moral stance in regard to unacceptable prejudice. Robert's father, in turn, told him that his mother was needlessly depriving him of something he treasured. Caught up in their passionate arguments, neither parent considered that Robert had no way to weave these opposing views together into some coherent understanding and so were unable to find a way to address his dilemma (e.g., *"I have strong feelings about this matter; I know your dad/mom does, too; that puts you in a very tough spot trying to sort it out. There's probably something true about each of our perspectives.")*

In going back and forth between homes, children often voice complaints to one parent about the other—to let off steam, for instance, or because they hope they will get a strong reaction from the parent they complain to. Usually, complained-to parents fail to handle such complaints with the sort of equanimity the child requires because they are still affected by feelings about the ex-spouse.

> *Upon returning from a weekend with her father, Amy, ten, complained to her mother that her father spent most of Saturday afternoon watching college football. Her mother responded, "Yeah, big surprise, that's one of the reasons I had to get out of the marriage."*

Optimally, a mother in this situation might say, *"That sounds hard. Did you try to let your dad know how you felt about it?"* However, Amy's mother, caught up in residual feelings from the marriage, was unable to speak to Amy's feelings about her father's lack of availability or help Amy problem-solve. Over time, Amy came to feel that there was no real point in speaking to her mother about frustrating features of life at her father's home and stopped doing so. She also became aware that her own needs were secondary to her mother's drive to express unhappiness with Amy's father. More ominously, Amy might come to feel that complaining about her father would be the most reliable avenue for connecting emotionally with her mother and the quality of her relationship with her father may erode. Alternatively, she may come to feel estranged from her mother because her mother refuses to support her relationship with her beloved (if frustrating) father.

Children, in addition to issuing their own complaints, often report back to one parent complaints that the other parent made. Unfortunately, when complained-about parents defensively state their side of the story—a natural response—their vision of what the child needs at the moment is clouded. A girl might say to her father: "Mom said she left you because you are so angry all of the time." The father might respond: "That's ridiculous, she left because she would rather hang out with her friends." Children in these circumstances feel caught between parents' differing accounts and criticized parents often feel stuck: They want to defend themselves yet recognize that doing so does not help them connect with their children. The kind of emotional equilibrium parents would need in order to offer a calm response is probably impossible when they remain bound up emotionally with a former partner; it would require instead the relative dispassion one would find in a parent who has progressed through a constructive mourning process.

THE IMPACT ON CHILDREN OF OVERT CONFLICT

It is amazing to observe how some people who exert expertise in challenging domains—building a house or, literally, doing brain surgery—cannot find simple solutions to avoid unpleasant struggles with a spouse or ex-spouse. While such struggles are most inflamed in the high-conflict divorce, they can undermine the quality of family life even in less conflicted divorces. Overt conflict reflects parents' inability to disengage. Like other features of life in families of divorce, the amount of conflict fits on a spectrum, ranging from none or almost none to the type of protracted battling one sees in the high-conflict divorce.

Children often feel overwhelmed by parents' arguing (and, even more, by physical fighting) around divorce. Indeed, many young adults remain seared by memories of their parents' confrontations, the intervening years having done little to ameliorate their anguish at witnessing bitter, sometimes violent parental interactions (Wallerstein, 1989). Parents underestimate the impact on children of overt conflict when they view it through adult eyes, failing to recognize how overstimulated and frightened children feel when parents battle. Children, especially babies, toddlers, and preschoolers, are much less able than adults to integrate intense stimuli without feeling overwhelmed, even traumatized. Some children want to intervene in the parental conflict. If they do, they are confronted with a painful experience of helplessness.

Besides being overstimulated, children's esteem for their parents drops when their parents behave badly because it is hard to admire parents who are feuding like children on a playground. The issue can be framed in Kohut's selfobject terms (see chapter 1): Children want and need to admire their parents in order to feel good about themselves. When parents squabble, that need may be thwarted, and children lose something essential. Parents' stability and maturity orders the world and reassures children that competent, steady adults can manage themselves and the child. In the face of parents' lapses, children worry that they are no longer on their parents' radar; some feel that they themselves cannot be contained and wonder if they will act out impulsively like their parents.

Sasha, twelve, talks in therapy about her parents' behaviors since their divorce. They often belittle each other. In addition, each has engaged in serial romantic relationships that, like the marital relationship, descended into angry squabbling. Sasha wonders why she should even try to behave herself when the grown-ups behave badly. She accuses her parents of being hypocritical when they set limits on her. She tells them with some justification: "You can't even manage yourselves. Why do you think you can manage me?"

PROBLEMATIC PARENTING ARRANGEMENTS

Parents sometimes put parenting arrangements in place that strain children unnecessarily. As one important example, some parents implement 50/50 parenting arrangements in order to resolve disputes between them (Macoby and Mnookin, 1992). While such an approach might help to diminish the need for continued litigation, splitting time evenly between two households when parents are tense with each other creates an especially large strain on children. Neil Kalter (personal communication) concluded that 50/50 parenting is viable only under certain conditions: Both parents have to want it, they have to be able to cooperate amicably, and the children need to be able to manage it. Other experts (e.g., Emery, 2012; Folberg, 1991; Waters and McIntosh, 2011) agree that a 50/50 arrangement should be put into place only under very specific conditions. As another example, parents often insist on frequent transitions between households even when every transition is hard on a child.

Parenting arrangements can become another forum in which parents' absorption in their own emotional experience trumps consideration of children's needs. For instance, when parents are determined that parenting arrangements be "fair," they really mean fair to the adults, not the children. A press for fairness emanates from unresolved feelings from the marriage and divorce: parents who feel they have been ripped off by the ex-spouse and seek redress in a particular parenting arrangement without fully considering its impact on the children. Parents might try to justify their investment in a particular arrangement in terms of children's needs, even when scrutiny indicates that children's needs are not being met. Some parents find bolstering in support groups. For instance, some father's rights groups argue that fathers have the right to equal time with their children. Such a stance focuses on parents' needs, not children's. While it may be in a child's best interest to have equal time with a father, in a given situation, it may not.

A common and troubling instance occurs when parents (with the sanction or even the mandate of the court) implement parenting arrangements that lose sight of young children's vulnerability to separations from a primary caregiver, often at a huge emotional price to the child.

Ms. Waters had arranged her work life so she could function as the primary caregiver of Marie, five. Mr. Waters, a successful businessman, spent limited time at home. After the divorce, Mr. Waters moved four hundred miles away to pursue a new job. He insisted that Marie see him for four-week blocks, an arrangement with which the court agreed, believing this little girl needed extended time with her father. Ms. Waters reluctantly agreed to give it a try in an effort to avoid conflict. After the first extended visit, Marie became symptomatic, crying frequently, clinging to her mother, and refusing to sleep.

Professor Akers and Ms. Akers had two sons together: Kyle, eleven, and Ryan, two. While they were married, Ms. Akers functioned as the primary caregiver as Professor Akers worked long hours. When they separated, they agreed it would be best for the children to have more time with their father, who was eager to reduce his administrative hours and spend more time parenting. Ms. Akers, eager to begin a new career, welcomed increased time to work. The parents put into place an arrangement in which the children went with their father weekly from Sunday morning until Tuesday afternoon. Kyle was delighted to have more time with his father. Ryan, however, was severely stressed by being away from his mother. He often was up crying at night and became increasingly morose.

Mr. Waters's press for extended visits with Marie ignored her developmental needs. Professor and Ms. Akers' wishes to keep the siblings together and create a schedule that attended to their own needs—not unreasonable on the surface—failed to take heed of Ryan's vulnerability to separations. Some parents, worried about escalating tensions if they try to readjust their parenting arrangement, fail to make changes to accommodate their children's evolving developmental needs.

Professionals working with divorcing families may make inappropriate recommendations for parenting arrangements if their own emotional conflicts, like those of parents, interfere with their ability to address children's needs or because they, too, fail to understand children's development. A colleague who worked for many years in a Friend of the Court office observed that some court personnel feel so guilty about recommending limited parenting time for one parent that they recommend shared parenting even when it increases the strain on children. Such an actuality highlights the powerful emotional forces at play in divorce situations that can interfere with a thoughtful assessment of children's need, even by people on the periphery of the family.

DENIGRATION OF THE OTHER PARENT

Some divorcing parents, caught up in bitterness, make contemptuous remarks about the other parent in front of the children. Children, for whom this sort of behavior is confusing and hurtful, are forced into stark confrontation with their parent's lapses in empathy and may come to feel disillusioned and cynical. They wonder, usually privately: How can you speak badly to me about my mother/father when you know that I love that person? How can you lose track of my feelings?

While denigration of the other parent is most overt and toxic in the high-conflict divorce, it, too, exists along a spectrum and can appear in more subtle ways in less highly conflicted divorces.

A mother, deeply hurt by her ex-husband's affair, made frequent comments to her sons about the importance of loyalty. She spoke about how "good men" stay faithful, and about how she hoped her sons would be "good men." While she did not specifically mention her ex-husband's affair, her sons, eleven and fifteen, understood the reference. Already disturbed by their father's behaviors, they felt even more torn between the parents because of her comments.

Denigration of the other parent is perhaps the most destructive manifestation of parents' emotional reactions to divorce undermining their empathy. Caught up in anger, parents fail to recognize that maligning the other parent places children in a bind: They must either ally themselves with the views of the denigrating parent or reject the denigrating parent for behaving badly.

CHILDREN IN THE HIGH-CONFLICT DIVORCE

The troubling features of ordinary divorces are accentuated profoundly in high-conflict divorces when beleaguered and embittered parents turn to their children to provide the selfobject functions they have lost in the spouse. By using children to bolster their flagging self-esteem, parents treat their children as extensions of themselves, losing track of their children's unique qualities. In addition, by seeking to draw their children into alignment with their own defensively driven perspectives on the marriage and divorce, parents place them under enormous psychological pressure, showing little or no empathy for their need to maintain positive relationships with both parents. Put differently, parents' urgent need to manage intolerable affects takes precedence over their children's emotional needs.

Children of furiously feuding parents find their parents' conflicting accounts of the marriage and divorce intolerable. They cannot understand how the two people they love the most—and whom they rely upon to order the world—can hold such different versions of the same realities. The more starkly parents draw battle lines, the harder it is for children to feel that they can comfortably love one parent without provoking the other parent's allegation that they have been disloyal. These children can feel (and sometimes parents reinforce this feeling) that they are either for a parent or against him or her.

Johnston and Campbell (1988) and Johnston, Roseby, and Kuehnle (2009) offer rich, detailed accounts of the impact of the high-conflict divorce on children at different developmental stages. They note that some high-conflict parents are most tuned in to a child when that child shares a distorted vision of the other parent. In order to maintain a connection to the parent, the child, in essence, is asked by the parent to relinquish "integrity, reality testing, and even the child's emerging sense of morality" (p. 32).

> *Mark, ten, appears beleaguered and downcast as he reports to his therapist*
> *that his mother says his father is a bad parent. His mother is smart, so she*
> *must be right. But his father is nice and takes him to football games. His father*
> *says he is not a bad father, so he must be right, too. But they can't both be*
> *right. He thinks his mother must be more right than his father, but he likes his*
> *father. Mark sighs and remarks that he is too little to sort this all out.*

One wonders how long this little boy can tolerate those conflicting views before deciding to choose one parent over the other, even if doing so means giving up a more balanced perspective on his parents and losing his connection to one. Mark's parents, unable to see his dilemmas, cannot help him. Children like Mark, caught in the storm their parents are creating, tend to feel disregarded and hopeless about sorting out "the truth." A therapist, positioned outside the fray, can potentially help children like Mark find language for their binds and help them understand the reality of their family situation (see chapter 11).

Johnston, Roseby, and Kuehnle (2009) suggest that children caught in the high-conflict divorce struggle with four main concerns: What is true and not true? How can I keep myself and my parents safe? Who is to blame? Am I like the good parent or the bad parent? They suggest further that children's efforts to manage these concerns, as well as deal with their fearfulness, "are likely to result in entrenched patterns of feeling, perceiving reality, solving problems, relating to other people, and dealing with emotions" (p. 40). Because these children cannot rely on their parents, they tend to turn inward to deal with what feel like intractable problems, but because their internal resources tend to be meager, they have difficulty dealing with ambiguity and complexity.

> *A year after he stopped therapy, the therapist has another chance to see Mark*
> *when his mother brings him back for a consultation because of school prob-*
> *lems. Mark is no longer struggling actively to figure out which parent is right*
> *about the marriage and divorce. Instead, he has concluded that his mother is*
> *right and his father lies. He still sees his father on occasion but no longer*
> *engages with him affectionately.*

Children may be traumatized by the mutual abusiveness between parents that is so prevalent in the high-conflict divorce but often do not receive help. Confronted with parents who are unable to move on with their lives, they are apt to become cynical and distrustful.

Many parents who divorce have at least some tensions around child-rearing matters. They may feud around a small matter (who was supposed to pick up the child from soccer practice) or get stuck in larger struggles in which they have trouble reaching resolution. In situations of high conflict, however, parents' enmeshment in an antagonistic relationship tends to preclude coordination of children's care, leading to untenable, even dangerous situations.

While still married, Ms. Bell becomes alarmed about her son, Jake, who is twelve. He appears withdrawn and depressed, spends most of his time playing video games, and rarely speaks to peers outside of school. She wants him to see a child psychiatrist and, perhaps, get antidepressant medication. Her husband scathingly dismisses her concerns. He believes his wife is just making excuses for Jake, whom he sees as simply lazy. In his view, Jake needs to get off his behind and get involved in sports or hunting. Mr. Bell opposes psychiatric consultation, viewing psychiatrists as "frauds" who make up maladies so they can get rich.

Post-divorce, the parents' disagreements about Jake escalate. Mr. Bell continues to insist that Jake needs more activities and, against both Jake's and his mother's wishes, signs Jake up for football. Ms. Bell makes an appointment for Jake to see a psychiatrist without informing Mr. Bell. When he learns of the appointment, he cancels it. The matter ends up in court. Ms. Bell has mobilized data, including a letter from the school counselor, to convince the court that Jake is depressed. Mr. Bell accumulates information to portray his ex-wife as hysterical and erratic.

An impasse of this sort can lead children to choose one parent and reject the other. While they must deal, then, with the loss of one parent, they can at least assure some stability of care (see chapter 10).

Chapter Six

The Effects on Adolescents of Parents' Difficulties in Navigating Divorce

ORDINARY CHALLENGES OF PARENTING ADOLESCENTS

Parenting adolescents can be challenging even in the most stable families. Adolescents often act as if they do not need parents, pushing them away in their efforts to assert autonomy and block out awareness of longings for closeness and nurturance that feel uncomfortably child-like. Most adolescents, appropriately, privilege relationships with peers, but many also use an immersion in peer relationships to keep their parents at arms' length. Modern technology—cell phones, the internet—contributes to teens' tendency to withdraw from more intimate engagement with adults.

Some parents buy into their teenagers' defensive pushing them away and mistakenly assume adolescents do not need parental guidance and intimacy. Other parents feel rejected by adolescents' pulling back and, without being aware of it, withdraw in turn because they feel hurt and confused. Pubertal girls often distance themselves from their fathers, no longer so sure about how to approach them as their bodies are changing; many fathers, reacting to that hesitancy and anxious themselves about their daughters' pubertal development, withdraw in turn. Neither father nor daughter quite has the language for what has happened; they just sense that something precious has been lost. Sadly, many parents assume that this is simply how it goes between parents and teens—that is, that they cannot connect in a meaningful way. Our culture's emphasis on autonomy and the need for individuation reinforces many parents' notion that they should give their teens more space to work things out for themselves.

Adolescents, as part of their gradual movement toward adulthood, need to "de-idealize" their parents, coming to see them more realistically as people

63

with both strengths and limitations. De-idealization can be painful for adolescents; it also is hard on parents, who feel diminished in their teenager's eyes. Some parents, worn down by angry adolescent protests against parental limit-setting, back away from insisting upon day-to-day structure and discipline around such critical issues as homework, curfews, and substance use. Parents are vulnerable to overlooking how urgently adolescents need adult guidance around the issues with which teenagers grapple: sexuality, peer relations, schoolwork, and morality. When adolescents and adults drift apart, adolescents are much more at risk for acting-out behaviors that imperil them and derail their development. But, in fact, most adolescents, although they are unlikely to admit it, appreciate when parents contain them in situations when they are unable to contain themselves by setting curfews and establishing consequences for rule breaking.

Optimally, adolescents begin to establish competence outside the home: in peer relationships, including romantic relationships, as well as school and work. When homes are stable and provide a sense of security, they serve as a kind of springboard, providing a safe, supportive space from which adolescents and young adults can propel themselves out into the world. Young people need to be able to return to the home for guidance and support, then engage energetically again out in the world (not unlike toddlers, who venture away from the parent, then return for "refueling").

In order to parent effectively and maintain intimacy with their teens, parents need to be on top of their game. They need to maintain high levels of energy in order to keep reaching out to an adolescent who is rejecting them, continually generating hope that their efforts will bear fruit. They need to be willing to stay in touch with the parents of their adolescent's peer group to ensure that the teens are doing what they say they are doing (even when the adolescent complains that such behavior is embarrassing and *no other* parent is doing it). They have to be willing to bear the slings and arrows of an angry adolescent's verbal assaults when the parent takes away car privileges after the adolescent breaks curfew. They have to be willing to go online and make sure the homework the teen is doing is, in fact, completed. They have to be willing to go ahead with vacation plans, even when teenagers say the plans are "stupid" and they would rather hang out with a boyfriend or girlfriend. Parents also need to be in close communication with each other and make sure that a wily adolescent does not play one against the other in an effort to gain more freedom. They have to be willing to talk about sex and drugs and be willing, at least at times, to listen to their teenager's music, even if they find it incomprehensible. Many parents find parenting teenagers to be deeply rewarding, even if exhausting and, at times, bewildering.

ADOLESCENTS AND DIVORCING PARENTS

Adolescents, already struggling to come to terms with their parents' limitations, are forced to confront these limitations more forcefully when their
parents' marriage falls apart. Because adolescents realistically *can* handle
more than younger children, and it is reasonable to ask them to pick up some
of the slack in a stressed post-divorce household (e.g., driving a sibling to a
music lesson or cooking a few times each week), it is easy to forget how
much they cannot manage. Adolescents, for instance, often find the sudden
exposure to their parents' sexuality when parents start dating to be confusing
and upsetting. Adolescents also can face unsettling pressure when they are
asked to participate in decisions about living arrangements: While they may
appreciate having a say, they also can feel burdened by a sense of guilt if
they feel they are rejecting one parent. Parents and adolescents sometimes
collude unconsciously to create scenarios in which the adolescent appears to
be managing but, in fact, is floundering.

An Ideal Approach to Co-Parenting Adolescents

Ideally, divorcing parents would sit down with their teenager and discuss
calmly and clearly what is going on in the family and what the teenager
might expect. Parents would include teenagers in discussions of possible
parenting arrangements. Many adolescents are concerned about potential dis-
ruptions to peer relations and extracurricular activities. Divorcing parents
would explore these concerns sensitively and work to create a parenting
arrangement that supported the teenager's school, social life, and interests.
While recognizing the teenager's needs, parents would not simply let a teenager's wishes hold sway—potentially encouraging a sense of entitlement—
but would balance these wishes against the needs of the parents and family as
a whole. After the parents separate, they would monitor their teenager carefully as they would their younger children to ensure she or he was managing
the emotional fallout of the divorce, keeping a careful eye on possible signals
of trouble, including a downward shift in school performance, inattention to
grooming, social isolation, or evidence of substance abuse.

At least as much as they would with younger children, responsible divorced parents of teenagers would share information so the teenager does not
fall into cracks between the two households. Because adolescents can quickly raise the stakes and get into serious difficulties, divorced parents would
stay in close touch and immediately share concerns (e.g., a fourteen-year-old
girl invited on a date by an eighteen-year-old boy). In the face of problematic
behaviors, divorced parents would quickly come together to support each
other's interventions, including consequences for rule breaking. If a sixteen-
year-old boy lost driving privileges for a week because he came home an

hour past curfew at his mother's house, his father would not let him drive at his house during that week either. They also would agree on rules that bear on issues of safety: for example, no more than one passenger in the car of a new driver, no sleepovers without assurance that parents will be home.

Adolescents in Danger

While facing the same predicaments around divorce as younger children, adolescents face developmental challenges that can make divorce especially difficult, even dangerous. These include the harsh reality that distressed adolescents can get into serious trouble fast. Hetherington and Kelly (2002) found that a higher percentage of early maturing girls from divorced homes (65 percent) were likely to have sexual intercourse at age fifteen than those from non-divorced homes (40 percent). The authors add that because early teenage sex is correlated with higher rates of sexually transmitted disease and pregnancy, adolescent girls from divorced homes are more likely to face these hazards.

Wallerstein (1989) found that that the breakdown of family structure after divorce leaves many adolescents adrift.

> *Nina, sixteen, comes to therapy depressed and withdrawn. Though she has managed to maintain high grades, she has been cutting her arms and legs and sneaking alcohol into school. Her mother, anguished about her divorce two years prior and overwhelmed by economic strains, has been unable to keep track of her troubled daughter. Nina, for her part, is worried about her mother's suffering and does not want to burden her further. Nina's mother finally recognizes the extent of the problem when Nina confesses that she is contemplating suicide. Nina's father, whom Nina sees only sporadically, is unaware of her acute distress.*

Wallerstein (1989) found that in the divorced families she studied, one of three males and one in ten females between the ages of nineteen and twenty-three got into trouble with the law. She viewed these adolescents primarily as "saddened" by the experience of abandonment and rejection by their parents. When they shifted from sadness to anger, as adolescents are prone to do, they got themselves into difficulties. She writes:

> [Some] youngsters after divorce feel there is no one in charge, no adult to make or enforce rules, no one to insist on proper conduct, and, perhaps most of all, no one to take over in an emergency. This sense that no one was in charge comes up repeatedly in our ten-year follow-up interviews. Children speak of empty homes, of needing adult guidance in protecting them from their own impulses, and of having too much responsibility for themselves and for younger children (p. 201).

One could add to this account that adults, understandably, have a hard time with angry adolescents, feeling put off by obnoxious behaviors and hostile attitudes. Parents' focus on anger (and angry acting out), while necessary, often means that teens' underlying sadness does not get addressed. Adolescents may be at greater risk than younger children in this regard because their modes of expressing distress can be especially aversive.

Barriers to Adolescents' Age-Appropriate Separation

It is much easier for young people to feel comfortable engaging energetically out in the world when their parents are flourishing because they know their parents do not *need* them to stay close, whereas parents who are hurting, sometimes for years, often turn to their adolescent and young-adult children to fill the void and provide a caregiving function. For an empathic, loving teen or young adult, caring for a needy parent can provide feelings of gratification and genuine accomplishment. Wallerstein and Kelly (1980) suggest, too, that such a role can increase a young person's capacity for empathy. However, young people's absorption in parents' distress can impede their separation process. Not only can caring for a parent take precedence over such age-appropriate concerns as extra-curricular activities, but young people tend to feel wracked with guilt when they feel they are leaving a grieving parent behind and wonder how they can have a thriving, lively life when a parent is bereft.

> Cory, seventeen, seeks therapy because he is unable to engage school with the diligence of which he is capable. Though bright, he consistently gets Cs because he does not concentrate. He plays video games instead of studying and smokes marijuana daily. His father, bereft, does not date and has given up on finding new love. His mother is unemployed and depressed. In therapy, Cory, who was desperately trying to block out awareness of his grief, is shocked to discover that he is unable to discuss his parents' plight without weeping. He considers dropping out of school to take care of them rather than leaving them behind by moving on with his life. He feels paralyzed.

In addition to inducing guilt, households in which the parents are flailing are less able to provide the emotional and material support that young people need in order to venture forth comfortably from home.

YOUNG ADULTS AND DIVORCING PARENTS

Young adults still need parental input in order to manage the myriad challenges of their lives, especially the challenging transition out of the parents' home. Some parents believe that late adolescents and young adults, once they leave home, ought to be able to manage essentially on their own. Young adults often reinforce this idea by assuming a stance of autonomy, even when they need assistance. They urgently want to be self-sufficient, when in reality they are not prepared to manage on their own. Any therapist (or parent) who deals closely with twenty- and twenty-one-year-olds knows well that this stance of independence often is paper thin. In addition to material support, young adults need guidance, reassurance, nurturance and, sometimes, limits. They usually appreciate the support and wisdom of grown-ups who have been confronted by similar challenges and can share ways to manage them.

Divorcing parents of young adults often need their young-adult children to function at a higher level than the young adult is able. If the parents have younger children, they typically focus on them. Young adults often throw themselves into college or work and function on the surface as if the divorce were something going on elsewhere that does not really affect them. Below the surface, though, they often feel as if their worlds were coming apart.

Tim, a college senior, immersed himself even more energetically in water polo and academics when he learned about his parents' divorce. His mother, aware that he might be affected by the divorce, pressed Tim to see a therapist. Tim initially insisted that the divorce did not really matter. After all, he had a girlfriend and was gearing up to apply to graduate school. However, as he pondered, he realized sadly that he did not even know which parent's house he would go to for the holidays.

ADOLESCENTS IN THE HIGH-CONFLICT DIVORCE

Ms. Cruz and Serena are locked into the typical miserable battles between a mother and a fourteen-year-old daughter. Ms. Cruz insists that Serena be home by ten on the weekends, for instance, and Serena complains bitterly that her mother is destroying her social life and is the only mother who has such ridiculous rules. They argue back and forth. Ms. Cruz asks Serena's father for support. However, instead of backing her, he retorts that he knows exactly what Serena is dealing with because he had to deal with the same "controlling crap" when he and Ms. Cruz were married. He tells Serena the same thing.

Serena's father, enveloped in bitterness, was unable to keep track of Serena's needs for a unified parenting front that could contain her. Optimally, even if he disagreed with his ex-wife, he would either support her or work with her privately (without including Serena, at least at the outset) to come to an agreement. In such a situation, Ms. Cruz and Serena may be unable to resolve their tensions, with potentially damaging consequences for their relationship and Serena's adolescent development.

While such conflicts occur with some regularity in more ordinary divorces, they are the norm in high-conflict divorces. Adolescents, prone to driving a wedge between parents in the best of circumstances, find ample reinforcement in their parents' bitter divide. Johnston, Roseby, and Kuehnle (2009) suggest that, because of a lack of coordination between households and parents' competition for adolescents' affection, adolescents in the high-conflict divorce can easily dismiss one or both of their parents or manipulate them to gain special privileges.

Adolescents, worn down by chronic discord, often relinquish a more balanced view of their parents' situation by aligning with one parent's black-and-white version of events, even if doing so means compromising their nuanced thinking.

> *Davis, eighteen, a college freshman, was asked to participate in a custody evaluation involving his younger brothers. He proudly told the evaluator that he saw the world in black and white terms and did not like gray. Davis described how he used to be confused about which parent was lying. Two years ago, however, he finally realized "the truth": His mother was honest and his father lied.*

In the course of interviewing Davis, it became clear he had been living with intolerable pressure since the parental separation during his early teens. His mother had been furious at him when he chose to visit his father. In turn, his father had told him that his mother was a "nut job." Therefore, he could not find a comfortable, safe space in either household. In addition, as hard as he tried, Davis could not figure out whose version of reality was more accurate. By choosing one "truth," Davis adaptively consolidated a close relationship with his mother (though sacrificing a relationship with his father). His reductionistic approach to a complicated family situation came at the expense of his cognitive integrity.

Part II

INTERVENING

*HOW THERAPISTS CAN
FACILITATE MOURNING*

Chapter Seven

Bearing Feelings, Facilitating Mourning

SOME DILEMMAS OF "AMBIGUOUS" LOSS

Loss in the case of death is not ambiguous. When a loved person dies, we as a society have typical prescribed rituals that take heed of the impact of the loss: funerals, time off from work, condolence notes (Betz and Thorngren, 2006). In order to address loss, people need external confirmation of its reality. Otherwise, a defensive denial is likely to hold sway—a minimization or refutation of loss. Writing of the need for social support in response to death, Fowlkes (1991) writes:

> In the absence of reliable patterns of support from others the mourner may come to doubt the meaning attached to the loss and to distrust the legitimacy of grief itself; it is but a small step from the inner confusion and uncertainty generated by social indifference or blindness to loss to self-blame and protracted grieving associated with melancholia (p. 533).

Rituals in response to death serve such a confirmatory function, explicitly acknowledging that a major loss has occurred. These rituals offer space for what Bowlby (1980) has suggested is essential to the person who has suffered a loss: the acceptance and encouragement of expressions of grief. Rituals in response to death also function to support the mourner by attending to key elements of the environment (food, financial needs, burial) that the mourner him- or herself is unable to attend to (Hagman, 1996).

Other losses, such as those that inhere in miscarriage, migration, chronic illness, the end of relationships and divorce, are more *ambiguous* and, therefore, often are not recognized and legitimized by society (Betz and Thorngren, 2006). These authors suggest that the lack of rituals for mourning in ambiguous loss renders the loss less tangible, impeding the mourning process. The losses in divorce are not always front and center because divorce often includes dramatic controversies, stunning betrayals, misunderstandings, simmering tensions over property and custody, explosive arguments, courtroom confrontations, even physical fights. While disturbing, these elements of divorce can fascinate. (One might think in this context of the excitement and intrigue generated by celebrity divorces.)

The dramatic turmoil surrounding divorce can distract the parties involved and others in the environment from acknowledging devastating losses and thereby reinforce family members' defenses against mourning. In the absence of social support, people in mourning are prone to feel they are being "silly or self-indulgent" and fear they are embarrassing or imposing on others (Schlesinger, 2007, p. 121). In addition, unlike the rituals that surround loss by death, loss by divorce rarely brings the kind of material support (such as food) that helps create a space to grieve.

Divorcing grown-ups often have no idea how to bear grief; some do not even know they *are* grieving. Children in distress rarely have the words for their sorrow and anger and most divorcing parents lack means for helping them deal with their troubling feelings. We can think of the people, then, who approach therapists for help around divorce—an adult consumed with bitterness, a child acting out angrily at school, a parent and child unable to connect emotionally—as stuck or partially stuck around the tasks of mourning. We can conceptualize a central therapeutic task, then, as facilitating mourning or, in the case of parents, helping them to facilitate their children's mourning.

HOW DOES TALKING HELP?

The Jewish tradition of shiva provides concrete assistance and a "context of care" within which a person who has lost a loved one to death can begin to mourn (Slochower, 1993). Slochower's focus on the interpersonal context of mourning in the rituals of shiva resonates with that of psychoanalytic writers who suggest that a caring, empathic environment not only facilitates mourning but is necessary for mourning to occur (e.g., Furman, 1974; Hagman, 1995a; Hagman, 1996). How does a person facilitate mourning?

In exploring the crucial need for communication between parents and children around children's experience of divorce, Kalter (1990) enters the complex territory that lies at the heart of this question: the mechanisms through which interactions between two people make a difference. To feel sad or anxious about a divorce is bad enough, Kalter writes, but to feel isolated in distress is unbearable. Being understood helps a person feel less alone. Kalter adds a crucial piece to this discussion by noting that the capacity of grown-ups such as therapists or parents to speak openly and calmly to a child's disturbing feelings communicates that the distress is not quite as overwhelming and unmanageable as the child imagined. The grown-up's genuine efforts communicate a model for confronting problems and offer hope that difficult feelings can be managed. In addition, open lines of communication allow parents to clarify children's misconceptions about divorce.

When caregivers attune themselves sensitively to children's range of affective experiences, children can integrate these experiences into their sense of self. Conversely, an absence of steady, empathic attunement leads to a defensive need to disavow these experiences because they threaten the sense of self. Shane and Shane (1990) suggest that children are spontaneously propelled to mourn—to think, talk, and reflect upon loss—*if* supportive others help the child bear pain. But their movement toward mourning is thwarted when grown-ups present criticism and "unrealistic standards for mourning behavior" (p. 119).

We can suggest that the mechanisms for facilitating mourning in adults are similar. Adults need a concerned, understanding other to help them to bear grief and to offer a model for how painful feelings can be borne. In examining the aftermath of loss, Tessman (1996) writes:

> Although the support of others can neither change nor undo whatever degree of pain is associated with the parting, its presence, like symbolic comforting arms, may help make the pain bearable enough to be experienced as such, rather than disguised or distorted into forms which in the long run may be more debilitating to the individual (p. 31).

People who grow up with non-empathic responses to painful emotional experiences in their early environment come to anticipate non-empathic responses later; accordingly, they will be reluctant to engage with others around conflicted emotional experiences. Assumptions about others' incapacity to tolerate difficult feelings infiltrates therapy when our patients feel highly skeptical that therapists can do what, perhaps, no one ever has done with them before: bear their painful feelings.

FACILITATING THE INTEGRATION OF PAINFUL FEELINGS

Elizabeth Marquardt (2005), in her account of growing up with divorce, shares a vignette that captures beautifully the emotional dilemmas of children in divorce and the potential impact of an understanding adult. She describes an interaction she had with an aunt when she was twenty-three years old. Her aunt observed aloud that she (Marquardt) had always seemed grown-up as a girl, remarking, "When you were five years old, you talked just like a grown up." Marquardt had heard such compliments about her maturity her whole life. However, her aunt added something markedly different, "I always thought it was kind of sad" (p. 33). Marquardt froze at those words because they were so different from the ordinary platitudes she heard from grown-ups. When her aunt spoke aloud about how sad this was, Marquardt saw her five-year-old self through her aunt's eyes and realized that, indeed, it *was* sad she had acted so mature as a little child. Her mother, absorbed in post-divorce stresses, and her father, often far away, had never affirmed how burdened and even overwhelmed she felt growing up in two households.

Marquardt's reflections highlight typical barriers to constructive mourning in relation to divorce. Marquardt herself blocked out awareness of her sorrow about having to act more grown-up as a girl than she actually felt—perhaps because she experienced her sadness as a condemnation of her parents whose self-absorption left her feeling alone, or, perhaps, because she found her sorrow too intense to bear without help. Her brief account suggests that the adults in her environment not only colluded with her defensive disavowal of her sorrow but reinforced it by praising her for being so grown-up, which apparently meant managing her parents' divorce without unbecoming (i.e., "childish") displays of emotion. They communicated their preference for dealing with a pseudo-mature child, as opposed to an overtly distressed child. Such responses exemplify the "unrealistic standards for mourning behavior" which self psychologists describe as obstructing children's mourning (Shane and Shane, 1990, p. 119).

Intent on evoking adults' admiration—and what child is not?—the little girl would have discerned, though not necessarily consciously, that adults around her had trouble tolerating manifestations of her sorrow. Whatever internal conflicts she had about acknowledging her sorrow would weave inextricably with influential messages from others to create a compelling need to present herself to the world—and to herself—as a stoical, super-mature girl. Until her aunt's comment, that is. Marquardt's aunt was able to see through her niece's pseudo-maturity, recognizing that it reflected a little girl's efforts to manage a stressful home environment. Her aunt's words affirmed that her composure was not admirable but, instead, was a sad commentary on life growing up in a household where she often had to take care of herself. Her aunt's permission to acknowledge her sadness appeared to help free Marquardt to begin to integrate disowned aspects of her reaction to her parents' divorce. Marquardt's strong reaction to her aunt's comment—her immediate feeling that her aunt was right—suggests she longed for another person to recognize the reality of her emotional experience. The interaction with her aunt poignantly captures, too, how, in the absence of empathetic others, it can be extremely difficult, if not impossible, to tolerate certain painful feelings.

THE EMOTIONAL DEMANDS ON THE FACILITATOR

Marquardt's aunt was able to see through her niece's outward stance of composure to recognize buried feelings. What does it take for a person to mobilize such an insight and speak it aloud? For one, it takes a capacity for affect tolerance. If our own sadness stirs anxiety such that we disown it, then we cannot bear another person's sadness because it stimulates awareness of our sadness, which in turn stimulates anxiety and concomitant defenses. Put simply, we can only tolerate feelings in others that we can tolerate within ourselves. Marquardt's aunt was able to bear her own sorrows sufficiently to tune herself in to her niece's underlying sadness, whereas parents who need to disown sorrow cannot facilitate its expression in their children. A therapist or family member stepping in from outside may be more tolerant of a child's grief and able to play a facilitating role. But that role, too, presents challenges. Parens (2001) writes: "We know that we cannot help a child deal with painful experiences without empathetically allowing the child's affects to resonate within our own psyche, with our own experiences of object loss, an experience unavoidably painful . . . for each of us" (p.161).

As part of her capacity to be responsive, Marquardt's aunt, apparently, did not have selfobject needs in relation to her niece that overrode her empathy: She did *not need* her niece to be a person she could admire for an ostensible capacity to manage challenges without undue distress. For other adults in Marquardt's childhood environment, such needs appeared to take precedence over a genuine wish and capacity to see that this girl was suffering. When a parent's selfobject needs are too great in relation to a child, a therapist might assume a role a parent cannot. For instance, a therapist might admire a child's courage in confronting his or her sorrow rather than denying it, offering an alternative vision of what constitutes "maturity."

Notably, Marquardt's aunt was unwilling to put her thoughts about the hard-edged reality of her niece's experience aside, but wanted to speak them aloud. Hagman (1996) contends that putting affects into words is crucial in the later stages of mourning, allowing for the ordering of inchoate affective experiences, which then can be integrated and worked with. Therapy offers a setting in which two people seek words for experiences which, to that point, have remained unspoken. Therapists' ability to work steadily and sensitively with their patients' defenses against conflicted feelings—which therapists must recognize and bear—gradually helps patients increase their own capacity to tolerate these feelings.

COUNTERTRANSFERENCE CHALLENGES

In working with divorce, therapists must find ways to see through a patient's defensive exterior and be willing and able to bear difficult feelings and risk rejection if the person we are speaking to pushes away our overtures. But because we as therapists have our own defensive needs to ward off disturbing thoughts and feelings, we, like some parents, can collude with our patients' defenses. Wallerstein (1990), writing on therapists' countertransference reactions to divorce, suggests that the collapse of marriage—the reversal of love into hate—stirs fears in therapists about our own intimate relationships. She suggests that we are caught between our wishes to be aware of our patients' suffering, thereby putting ourselves in touch with sorrow and anxiety, and our needs for psychological distance. In addition, I would suggest, we as therapists run the risk of being so absorbed in our own narcissistic (selfobject) needs in relation to our patients that we can lose sight of their needs. For instance, if we need our patients to progress steadily and look increasingly composed in order to affirm our adequacy as therapists, we easily miss the impact of their continuing internal struggles and risk being one more person in a their environment who needs them to be a certain way (e.g., to flourish).

Therapists must be willing to take emotional risks, then, in order to help patients deal with their feelings about divorce.

> *Kevin, fourteen, was brought for a consultation by his parents because they were concerned that he had increasingly withdrawn from the family to listen to angry hip-hop music in his room in the months following their divorce. When the psychologist asked about how the divorce affected him, Kevin, sullen and defiant, responded that he did not "give a shit" about the divorce because he had his own life, different from his parents'. He said that therapy was "stupid" because he was managing okay.*

The therapist sensed that this teenager was suffering greatly. However, he felt shut down by Kevin's dismissive response to his query about the divorce. He considered, briefly, that his sense that Kevin was in distress might be wrong and thought about pulling back from talking about the divorce, but he recognized that he was becoming self-protective and moving toward withdrawal in the face of rejection. Gaining his bearings by staying tuned in to his sense that Kevin was despairing, the therapist persisted, saying to Kevin, "I understand you have your own life and you have created a safe space in your room; at the same time, all teenagers are affected, at least a little, by what's going on with parents." The "at least a little" comment reflected the therapist's understanding that Kevin, blocking out strong reactions to the divorce, would need to shut him down if he suggested that Kevin was affected a lot. By talking about "all teenagers," the therapist hoped to normalize the experience and diminish Kevin's sense of shame at being so reactive. Toward the end of the third interview, Kevin briefly acknowledged he had been depressed for eight months, which, though he did not articulate it, was when his parents told him they were divorcing.

It would have been more comfortable for the therapist to accept Kevin's stance of nonchalance or his defiance toward his parents and never gain access to—and have to bear—his sorrow. Had the therapist not counteracted his own impulse to withdraw, he would have communicated that he, like Kevin, was unable to tolerate Kevin's depressive feelings and would have reinforced the teenager's sense that these feelings were unmanageable. While finding a way, gently, to speak to Kevin's suffering, the therapist stayed tuned in to Kevin's defenses, appreciating that Kevin needed to disown his depression for powerful reasons, including, it eventually turned out, a sense of shame that he was unmasculine for being so upset.

RESISTING THE PULL TO ALIGN WITH DEFENSES

Individuals who are determined to push away sorrow often enjoin others, including therapists, to ally with their defenses against underlying pain. Such pressure is most pronounced around the high-conflict divorce (see chapter 10), but is evident in all divorces. A divorcing individual who seeks to strengthen his or her defensive disavowal of, for example, feelings of shame, might seek to pull friends and family members into an angry discussion of the ex-spouse's character flaws. While such a buttressing provides necessary relief and is not harmful in and of itself, it becomes problematic if the angry conversations do not eventually allow some integration of sadness at loss. When people in the environment can resist the impulse to ally with the divorcing person's defenses, they can play an active role in facilitating mourning.

> *Ms. Damato became enraged during her divorce when she saw her husband walking down the street with a new girlfriend. She called her attorney in a fury, insisting that they go to court immediately, rather than continue with mediation. Her attorney, wisely, suggested that she cool off and reconsider. Later that day, Ms. Damato's therapist asked her if she could slow down and think about what she was feeling before she became so angry. Ms. Damato pondered, then began to cry. She spoke about how hurt she felt that her husband seemed to move on so easily with his life.*

Both Ms. Damato's attorney and her therapist served crucial functions. The attorney, instead of reinforcing her client's outrage, advocated calmness, understanding that Ms. Damato was flaring because she was upset about her husband's girlfriend and knowing that litigation would not serve her client well. Her therapist played a critical role by helping Ms. Damato think about the feelings that underlay her sudden fury upon seeing her husband.

Ms. Damato had the wherewithal to surround herself with people who could bear her distress. She selected a lawyer who was invested in mediation and did not jump to litigate when her client expressed outrage, as some family law attorneys do. If litigation forestalls mourning, as suggested, then non-adversarial modes of conflict resolution such as mediation and collabo- rative divorce serve to facilitate it (see chapter 10). Ms. Damato selected a therapist who understood that her fury served a defensive function. By asking what feelings had preceded her outburst, he helped her become aware of her underlying distress. Horowitz (1990) suggests that "preexisting neurotic character" interferes with some people's ability to use others for emotional support during mourning (p. 317). Others, like Ms. Damato, have the wisdom and emotional fortitude to bring people into their lives who can provide crucial support.

Researchers and therapists who deal with divorce risk losing track of family members' distress because these people's defenses are often so com- pelling that they create the illusion that loss was minimal. Marquardt (2005) argues that many such experts underplay the impact of divorce on children, especially when conflict is minimal. She decries the notion of the "good divorce," asserting that divorce is rarely good for children and that adults have their own needs to downplay children's excruciating emotional experi- ences.

Some divorce researchers question Wallerstein's conclusions about the devastating impact of divorce on children, adolescents, and adults, raising methodological concerns about her research. For instance, Kelly and Emery (2003) cite the relatively small and unrepresentative samples in Wallerstein's work. They also note that some studies confuse correlation with cause; some problems found in divorced families existed before the divorce occurred. Strohschein (2007) cites research that indicates that children of divorce are at a greater risk for mental health problems and greater instability in their intimate relationships. She notes, too, that research confirms that parents report greater levels of psychological distress and depression after divorce. At the same time, she writes that researchers have become more circumspect about the negative consequences of divorce in recent years. She questions whether divorced parents actually demonstrate what Wallerstein and Kelly (1980) referred to as the "diminished capacity" of parents to care for their children post-divorce.

Like Kelly and Emery, Strohschein makes the important point that some parents who show inadequate parenting after divorce were diminished as parents while married. At the same time, Strohschein employs broad behav- ioral categories of parenting ("nurturing" parenting, "consistent" parenting, and "punitive" parenting) along with simple numerical scales that cannot possibly address the critical (and sometimes subtle) lapses in parental empathy that I am describing in many of the clinical vignettes here. How often a parent and child laugh together or play together is not a measure of parents' capacity to attune themselves sensitively to a child's grief following a divorce.

Of course, divorced adults and children who present for treatment represent a subgroup of individuals that is much more likely to be acutely distressed than people involved in divorce who do not seek treatment, as Kelly and Emery (2003) note. In an effort to clarify divergences in the research findings of Wallerstein and those of researchers who are more sanguine about divorce, these researchers suggest that one needs to distinguish between emotional pain and pathology. In other words, while children of divorce may not show significantly higher levels of psychopathology, "divorce can create lingering feelings of sadness, longing, worry, and regret that coexist with competent psychological and social functioning" (p. 359). I would suggest that while such feelings of longing and sadness and worry and regret may not reach the threshold of psychiatric disorders, they still can play a formidable role in a person's sense of self and can profoundly influence intimate relationships.

Chapter Eight

Working with Parents Together to Help Children

THE IMPORTANCE OF INCLUDING PARENTS IN THEIR CHILDREN'S THERAPY

In their initial phone call to child therapists, parents alarmed about their child's emotional reactions to a divorce often request individual therapy for that child. Some hope a therapist can connect with the child in ways the parent is unable to. Others are aware that divorce-related difficulties are affecting the child but are hesitant to deal with their ex-spouse because doing so is so upsetting. They hope if a therapist meets with the child that at least *something* is being accomplished. However, because so many of the difficulties children face around divorce involve problems with parents, working with parents as well is essential. If parents have put a parenting arrangement into place that strains a child unduly, trying to help a child without addressing it misses the point. From a systems perspective, a focus on children's difficulties distracts attention from parents' inability to move toward a post-divorce adjustment that attends adequately to their children. Providing children with individual therapy when their parents are struggling to attend to them is like providing children caught in a thunderstorm the chance to talk about how wet they are. They might appreciate the empathy, but they are still wet and cold.

There are other reasons to keep parents involved in therapeutic work with children. As a culture, including our therapy culture, we often underestimate the crucial role that parents play in children's development. That idea may seem paradoxical, given our society's focus on the impact of parents on children. However, in our attention to children's individuation and establishment of autonomy, we often lose track of how much children need a close connection to their parents throughout their development. This oversight is common in regard to older children, especially adolescents. Therapists working within this cultural milieu often underestimate even younger children's need for intimacy with their parents and miss out on a critical function of therapy: improving the quality of parent/child relationships, especially important in divorce situations when parents and children have drifted apart.

When parents are not afforded the chance to express their points of view, especially when children are exaggerating parents' liabilities and denying their own contributions to family tensions, children can feel buttressed in their fury at parents and less inclined to self-reflect. While child therapists see it as their job to ally themselves empathically with children, which may mean allying with them *against* their parents, they need at the same time to avoid assuming that all of a child's complaints are undistorted and valid. Regular contact with parents allows for a more balanced view of the family situation.

The Pressure on Therapists to Exclude one Parent

Some divorced parents who call about child therapy do not mention the other parent or indicate, dismissively, that she or he does not play an important role in the child's life. Sometimes, of course, this is true. Often, though, one parent hopes to get help for the child without having to deal with the ex-spouse. It is rarely a good idea for a therapist to agree to meet with a child without consulting first with the other parent. If parents have joint legal custody, each has a legal right to decide if she or he wishes to support a child's therapy and a right to be included. In addition, it is hard for therapists to intervene constructively unless both parents participate.

I have seen situations in which therapists have worked with a child without ever talking to one parent (usually the father). The excluded parent felt justifiably upset; some even consulted lawyers. Therapists justified their treatment decisions in ways that strained common sense—for example, "I am working with the child, not the parents," or, "The father is the problem." How can these therapists know what is going on in the family without speaking to both parents? Such situations usually reflect therapists' succumbing to the countertransference trap of forming an alliance with one parent and so dismissing the other. While this sort of trap is most common and pernicious in the high-conflict divorce, it can lure therapists in situations with more modest levels of tension.

Many divorce-related circumstances that disturb children can be addressed most fruitfully through meetings with parents *together*. If I determine in the initial consultation that parent work is necessary, I ask parents if they can sit in the same room together. If they indicate that they cannot, I press gently. If they insist it is impossible, I let it go and proceed with individual parent sessions. Because violence is common around divorce situations, therapists should inquire about a history of violence at the outset because it usually is unwise to bring parents into the same space when there has been violence. If parents respond that they can meet together but it will be tense, therapists might let them know that they are prepared to deal with their tension. Doing so conveys that the therapist is not daunted by the parents' strong feelings, especially anger. It also conveys optimism in the face of their feeling helpless and hopeless.

STRUCTURING SESSIONS WITH BOTH PARENTS

Some Challenges of Two-Parent Sessions

In joint parent sessions, divorced parents must be willing to talk openly about the impact of the divorce on their children and open themselves up to therapists' interventions. They face what can feel like a cruel irony in that they split up because they were unable to resolve conflicts and now they are deliberately coming together in order to work out conflicts.

> *Dr. Khan shook her head in exasperation in the first appointment with her ex-husband to discuss the possibility of therapy for their son, Omar. She stated angrily, "Mr. Khan and I split up because we could not agree on anything. I still think he is a self-centered, immature man who cannot think about our children for more than a few minutes at a time. And you think we are going to have reasonable conversations about Omar's problems at school?" Mr. Khan energetically agreed with his ex-wife's pessimism, observing angrily that Dr. Khan never had respected him as a parent. Why would she start now?*

By bringing divorced parents together in an effort to intervene, therapists step between parents and have to bear the difficult feelings that derive from doing so. Therapists face a number of challenges: For instance, how do we carve out a middle space between two people who are vulnerable to feeling rejected and hurt if we do not align with their individual perspectives? In the session with Dr. Khan and her ex-husband, I struggled to maintain hope in the face of their pessimism. I worked to keep a vision of Omar in mind—his urgent need for his parents to work well together—which bolstered my morale. I also used the focus on Omar to carve out a space between the tense parents, reminding them (and myself) that all interventions would represent an effort at clarifying what their son needed, as opposed to addressing the *parents'* needs.

Establishing Ground Rules

Tense parents often have difficulty sticking to an agenda. They snipe at each other and bring up unresolved issues from the past. I reassure them that we will set a clear agenda for our meeting and I will enforce strict ground rules:

• No denigrating the other parent.
• No making gratuitous comments.
• No veering from the agenda at hand.

Therapists, in addition to being firm with ground rules, must be aware of parents' anguish over unresolved issues. When a marriage ends, especially suddenly, it can be excruciating for a person to be left without a chance to discuss with the spouse what happened. Sometimes a joint parent session, especially in the midst of a divorce, is the first time parents have been in close proximity since they separated and they are brimming with strong feelings.

While therapists need to acknowledge how hurt and angry parents feel, it is important that they explain that joint parent sessions are *not* a forum in which to address old conflicts from the marriage or separation. Therapists can go on to say that unresolved issues between the parents will remain unresolved and identify that as one of the sad, frustrating realities of divorce. Therapists might also speak to how hard it can feel to have to mourn the end of the marriage without sharing the mourning process with the ex-spouse, all the more so when each parent had relied on the other for emotional support.

While staying aware of parents' emotional dilemmas, therapists can still insist on sticking to the issues at hand:

> *Mr. Lyle and Ms. Lyle met to discuss therapy for their daughter, May, twelve, a year after their divorce. They immediately launched into a heated discussion of why they divorced and how the other parent was responsible for stressing May. The therapist said to the parents: "I know it's hard to sit here and not get into those old conflicts. You've never had a chance to sort them out and it's sad to think you never will. But you need to put those tensions aside so we can figure out what makes most sense for May." He added that the parents might need to find alternative venues to talk about their divorce-related frustrations.*

In working with May's parents as an adjunct to May's therapy, the therapist had to make similar interventions many times. Over the course of a year, though, the parents settled down considerably.

Staying Active

Some therapists, accustomed to the more receptive mode of individual therapy, allow parent sessions to slide out of control. When parent meetings escalate, parents lose faith in therapists, wondering how they can deal with challenging children if they cannot deal with parents. In a consultation that still distresses me to recall, I allowed a man to rage at his ex-wife on and off during a one-hour interview. The woman, who felt unable to manage her husband's fury during their marriage, felt unprotected in the parent session. Understandably, she chose not to return for further meetings. In working with parents, therapists have to be willing to assertively provide structure. In the situation described above, I needed to let this man know quickly that he needed to settle down or we could not proceed. It was a painful but valuable lesson.

Bearing Our Own Vulnerability

Many therapists feel emotionally vulnerable sitting with divorcing or divorced parents together. Accustomed to seeing primarily individuals, they tend to feel scrutinized in parent sessions—acutely aware that each parent is observing how the therapist interacts with the other. I find that I sometimes worry that one or the other parent will be unhappy. I work to sort out those feelings within myself so I do not withdraw from interacting energetically. Therapists can feel less burdened by divorced parents' expressions of unhappiness with parent sessions by keeping in mind that these parents, especially when they are tense, tend to feel that their views are being disregarded. In fact, in working with tense parents, I usually feel that I am doing a good job if *both* parents feel somewhat unhappy with me.

Staying Neutral

In working with tense divorced parents, therapists must be fastidious about appearing evenhanded, even if one parent is more provocative or challenging. Otherwise, they lose credibility and the ability to intervene. I often tell tense parents from the outset that each is likely to agree with some of my ideas and disagree with others. Anticipating this eventuality can help minimize its negative impact when it happens. I also work hard to avoid forming an alliance with one parent by staying as aware as possible of my emotional reactions to each parent. At the same time, I try to hold fast to my perceptions about what a particular child needs, even if articulating that perspective leads one parent to feel unhappy.

Offering Concrete Advice

Some child therapists hesitate to offer parents advice about what will help with their children. This hesitancy may be a residue from a model of individual therapy in which therapists tend to keep their opinions to themselves. But divorcing parents often feel completely lost about what to do with their children and seek concrete assistance, not just empathy. They want to know specifically what to say about a new girlfriend or specifically how much time a toddler can spend away from a primary caregiver. General suggestions are inadequate to such parents. In consultations, I have interviewed many parents who had met with therapists who failed to provide concrete guidance, which frustrated and confused them. They said in essence: If we could have figured this out for ourselves, we would not have taken the time and money to consult a therapist. Therapists who respond to parents' urgent requests for advice should be sure to frame their suggestions as just that, however, suggestions, and not to convey that they are offering definitive recommendations to which there are no alternatives.

As an adjunct to working with parents, a referral to a court-affiliated parent education program often is helpful. These programs seek to assist parents with different features of post-divorce parenting, including co-parenting conflict, parent-child relationships, and relitigation. A meta-analytic study of these programs found overall significant positive effects (Fackrell, Hawkins, and Kay, 2011).

If interventions with parents have no real effect and tensions continue unabated, therapists might advise parents to get a *parenting coordinator*, a professional who is appointed by the court to help them organize care in a more structured way (see chapter 10). Because parenting coordinators can communicate recommendations and concerns to the court, they can exert a lot more leverage than therapists who by definition practice in a confidential role. Gaining knowledge about how parenting coordinators function can help therapists explain to parents why engaging such a person could be helpful.

HELPING PARENTS PREPARE THEMSELVES AND THEIR CHILDREN FOR DIVORCE

Some parents, wishing to focus on their co-parenting relationship, seek consultation without their children. Some even ask therapists for assistance prior to divorcing in the hope of proactively alleviating as much stress as possible. Working with parents in advance of a divorce allows therapists a wonderful opportunity to provide simple interventions with potentially momentous ramifications. I suggest to parents that when they are ready to tell their children about the impending divorce they should meet with their children together. They should try to agree on as many details of future plans as possible and find a common language for explaining reasons for the divorce. If the parents are too tense to meet with the children together, they should meet with them separately, but they still should try to be on the same page in terms of concrete details and explanations for the divorce.

Hodges (1991) suggests that parents should talk about why the divorce is occurring, what is going to happen in terms of living space, when visitation will occur, and what will happen with holidays. Therapists can guide parents in framing their explanations in age-appropriate language and help determine what is more information than they should provide (e.g., that one parent is leaving because the other is having an affair). Helping parents guide their children in concrete ways—such as showing them the apartment building where the non-custodial parent will live—can significantly reduce children's anxiety (Wallerstein and Kelly, 1980). *Putting Children First* (Pedro-Carroll, 2010) offers detailed guidance for parents who are preparing their children for divorce.

Therapists can help parents set the stage at the outset for the sorts of important exchanges with their children that are so often missing when parents separate. For instance, they can suggest that parents, when they first speak to the children about the pending divorce, model ways of acknowledging and dealing with sad feelings: *"We really hoped we could work out our marriage but we can't. We both feel terribly sad about the divorce. We know that you will be awfully sad at times, too, in the days and months ahead. We have found that it is really helpful to talk to someone when we feel sad. Otherwise, we feel very alone. We very much would like to hear about your sadness about the divorce and any other feelings you have."* script

Parents can reassure their children that family members will get on with their lives and feel better as time passes but should not use this positive message to gloss over their children's difficult feelings. Parents often express anxiety about speaking directly about sadness, feeling they might be over-emphasizing the negative and making children feel worse. A therapist can let parents know that talking aloud about sadness not only does not *cause* children to be sad but the opposite is true: Children often need permission to feel sad and disappointed and feel worse when their feelings are unaddressed. I approach parents' reluctance in terms of *their* own difficulties with sad feelings, observing that it can be hard for parents to hear about their children's grief because it makes them feel guilty and sad themselves. Therapists, by providing a space in which parents can acknowledge and bear their own sorrow about the divorce, increase parents' capacity to be open to their children's feelings.

Wallerstein, Lewis, and Blakeslee (2000) offer nuanced, sensitive ideas about parent/child conversations about divorce that therapists can use to guide them. The authors recommend that parents speak to their children simply and slowly, keeping in mind that children will remember this initial conversation forever. They suggest that parents talk about the dreams they had together and how happy they were when the children are born, so that children feel they were born into a loving family and their parents wanted them. They recommend that parents describe how hard they fought for the script marriage and how reluctant they are to separate. The authors suggest that parents invite children to talk about what they know about divorce, so the parents understand the child's notions and, potentially, correct them. They believe parents should invite children to offer their own ideas about what would work for them so they do not feel like "inanimate objects that are just distributed between two homes" (p. 419). In addition, the authors recommend, parents should reassure their children that their planning will take account of the children's friendships and recreational activities.

By meeting with parents prior to the divorce, therapists can anticipate where difficulties will arise and problem-solve in advance. For instance, they can discuss with parents what sorts of plans they have devised for communicating with each other and can acquaint parents with the kinds of tensions that arise in post-divorce families and think about how the parents will address them. Therapists might arrange regular monthly or bi-monthly meetings with parents to help them deal with whatever challenges arise (e.g., one parent begins dating). They also might suggest that the parents find a school- or community-based program designed for children going through divorce.

HELPING TENSE PARENTS REDUCE CONFLICT

Feuding couples get stuck in patterns of conflict and use what ordinarily would be simple, practical transactions (e.g., who pays for a school trip) to grind axes or dredge up huge, unresolved issues, often pertaining to the disintegration of their marriage. Such discussions are rarely constructive and usually escalate into arguments. Collaboration falls apart and parents are left demoralized. Therapists can let parents know this.

From a more dispassionate perspective than parents can muster, therapists can offer ideas for moving forward more peacefully. Concrete suggestions are essential. If parents are bickering at transitions, a therapist might recommend that no issues be addressed spontaneously at pick-ups and drop-offs: The parents should politely say hello and nothing else. Whatever child-related issues parents need to discuss should be addressed before transitions and *without the children present.* Parents can establish regular times each week when they can talk by phone. If they are tense during these calls and begin to argue, they should set up a co-parenting agenda before the meeting using email and agree to discuss only what is on it.

While tense parents need advice that addresses logistical problems, they do not feud at transitions simply because they cannot figure out alternatives. Powerful emotional forces are at play that therapists can address. For example, a therapist might say: *"I know it is puzzling that you cannot speak spontaneously to each other about even simple matters without blowing up. You think, I can do it with other people, why can't I do it with my ex? But, for*

the time being that is how it is. It is a sorry truth that cannot be denied." ✱✱✱
Such an approach seeks to facilitate mourning because it addresses hard facts
the parents wish to deny and acknowledges underlying sadness and despair.
Any time we speak to difficult realities and underlying affects, we are chip-
ping away at parents' need to stay entrenched in fury. The intervention above
also addresses the parents' narcissistic vulnerability by stressing they are not
inadequate generally, just stuck in this one situation.

HELPING PARENTS COORDINATE CARE

Sometimes parents try to avoid discussing issues altogether because they so
easily slide into arguments. Therapists can press parents not to withdraw by
reminding them that they have a responsibility to their children to maintain
contact and articulating how hard it is for children to live in self-contained
households. Therapists can try to ameliorate the "between-two-worlds" experience of children by helping parents coordinate discipline so they maintain
similar expectations and consequences for misbehavior in both households
and also can get on the same page about schoolwork and other important
aspects of the child's life. By providing parents with a forum to speak with
each other so they have a better understanding of what life is like in the other
household, therapists help parents rely less on the child for information.

Sometimes one parent wishes to coordinate care in regard to such issues
as diet and homework and the other parent is unreceptive. While coordinating households can be helpful to children, each parent retains the option not
to for any number of reasons, including a concern that efforts at coordination
keep the ex-spouses too tangled up with each other and lead to more conflict.
Then joint sessions can be used not to coordinate care but, essentially, to
achieve the opposite result of drawing boundaries around households. A
therapist might tell tense parents that, within reason, each is entitled to parent
as she or he sees fit. The parent that seeks more coordination may need help
coming to terms emotionally with his or her limited influence over life in the
other household and may require concrete parameters for when intervention
in the other household is warranted.

HELPING PARENTS REFINE PARENTING ARRANGEMENTS

Options for Parenting Arrangements

Therapists working with divorcing families need to understand what parenting arrangements are appropriate for which children because, first, they must
be able to ascertain whether a particular arrangement is a source of difficulty
for a given child and, second, they must be aware of different options if they

are going to try to intervene when an arrangement is not working out. Options for parenting arrangements range from one extreme, where a child lives with one parent and essentially does not see the other parent, to the other, a 50/50 shared parenting arrangement. How parents come to an optimal parenting arrangement depends on a number of variables, including:

- The child's age
- The child's temperament
- The child's need for specialized services and the respective parent's ability to provide them
- The caregiving arrangements prior to the divorce
- The parents' current status (i.e., availability, motivation, work schedule)
- The level of conflict between the parents
- The child's stated preferences
- The child's logistical needs
- The quality of the relationship between each parent and the child

Therapists should understand that the field lacks consensus about these variables. Because parenting arrangements are sometimes fiercely contested and arouse strong passions (including politicized divisions along gender lines), there is often considerable controversy about what sorts of parenting arrangements are best for children. Such tensions can distract attention from the very difficult issues that come with trying to create optimal parenting arrangements.

Respected clinicians and researchers have offered sage, if sometimes inconsistent, recommendations for parenting arrangements that address children's psychological needs and provide a valuable resource for therapists. Kelly and Lamb (2000) use child development research to inform their recommendations regarding parenting arrangements for young children. Pruett, Ebling, and Insabella (2004) provide the results of their research on the impact of overnight visits for young children. Johnston, Roseby, and Kuehnle (2009) examine the stress of transitions on toddlers, highlighting the importance of rituals at transitions and bedtimes. Main, Hesse, and Hesse (2011) address parenting arrangements from the perspective of attachment theory, a rich theoretical framework, especially in regard to parenting arrangements for infants and toddlers. Hodges (1991) offers a detailed guide, organized by age, to designing thoughtful parenting arrangements. Johnston and Campbell (1988) and Emery (2012) stress that stability in schedules provides children with a much-needed sense of predictability when divorce disrupts established family routines. Pedro-Carroll (2010) offers detailed, straightforward advice to parents on creating thoughtful parenting plans.

Helping Parents Implement Minor Adjustments

When therapists ascertain that an existing arrangement is stressing a child, they can try to help the family manage it more smoothly. For instance, if the main difficulty for a child is parental conflict at transitions, and the therapist can help the parents reduce conflict, then a change in the actual parenting arrangement might be unnecessary. Sometimes a minor adjustment to an existing arrangement can make a big difference.

> *Cara, twelve, was seeing a therapist to help her manage her frustration about her parents' divorce, which had occurred five years earlier. She had been spending one evening each week and alternate Friday nights with her father. Cara explained to the therapist that she found the arrangement stressful because Friday night was the big social night among her middle school friends and her father lived thirty minutes away. Because the parents had maintained that arrangement for five years and worried that tensions that might arise were they to try to change it, they had left it alone. However, in consultation with the therapist, they agreed it would work best for Cara to spend alternate Saturday nights instead of Friday nights with her father.*

By suggesting a minor adjustment that alleviates strain on a child, a therapist offers a perspective that parents might lack because they are out of touch with their child or stuck due to inertia or conflict.

Even in an apparently simple situation such as this, therapists must tread gently because efforts at intervention must take heed of the feelings of all family members. Cara's mother might treasure having her daughter home on Saturday nights and object strenuously to a proposed change. A strict arrangement of confidentiality with a child—and isolating the therapy from the parents—would not work in an instance such as this. The therapist asked Cara's permission to speak with the parents about the Friday night dilemma and invited her to join a discussion with her parents. He also worked with her to become less inhibited in expressing her preferences to her parents by helping her see how worried she was about hurting one parent's feelings. Given that children and parents often drift apart, a critical part of the intervention is helping Cara be more in touch with her parents by speaking openly with them about her preferences.

Altering Parenting Arrangements More Significantly

If it becomes clear that a parenting arrangement is untenable and beyond repair, a therapist might suggest revising it altogether. However, therapists must exercise care because parents usually arrived at parenting arrangements through a (sometimes arduous) legal process and may cling to them tenaciously. One or both parents might be unwilling to make a change. Therapists can still share their opinion that an arrangement is not working. Parents retain different options: return to court, seek mediation, or do nothing at all. It is eminently reasonable for therapists to decide that dealing with parenting arrangements lies outside their domain of expertise or that getting embroiled with the parents in a potentially inflammatory matter would interfere with the child's therapy. If therapists decide to refer the parents, it is important for them to get to know specialists in the community (e.g., mediators) who are proficient at helping parents work out conflicts.

Considerations in Assessing Parenting Arrangements

When parents are tense, frequent transitions are more stressful for children, so the need for regular contact with both parents must be balanced against the cost of increased strain. In addition, children usually benefit from continuity, so it often makes sense for whichever parent was the child's primary caregiver prior to the divorce to continue in that role. That parent and child will likely have established a comfortable way of working together, so the child will feel most secure and comfortable in that routine. However, the idea of continuity should not be rigidly applied. Parents' lives change—there may be a new marriage, a new child, a new job—and children's needs change, too. Accordingly, parenting arrangements need to be re-evaluated on a regular basis.

Divorced parents who respond sensitively to a developing child's needs for change can have an enormous positive impact on that child's life.

> *Mike's parents divorced when he was seven years old. His mother, who had been his primary caregiver, continued in that role. Mike saw his father every Wednesday evening and alternating weekends. When Mike turned twelve, he began talking about spending more time with his father, whom he missed. In consultation with a therapist, the parents agreed to an arrangement in which Mike spent three days each week with his father. Both parents felt comfortable with this arrangement and the therapist felt that the parents could put the new arrangement into place without undue tension.*

Both of Mike's parents were aware that he was having a hard time not seeing his father more and were open to considering changes. If either parent had been opposed, it is unlikely that the therapist could have intervened.

Parents of young children need to pay special attention to parenting arrangements that strain them unduly because of too-long or too-frequent separations from their primary caregivers. Therapists can help parents understand how a young child's emotional/behavioral difficulties—fussiness, clinging behaviors, outbursts—can result from an ill-conceived parenting arrangement.

At the time of their divorce, Dr. Morris, a research professor, and Mr. Morris, a homemaker, put into place a parenting arrangement in which their daughters, six and three, lived about half of the time with each. Although Dr. Morris had been an involved parent prior to the divorce and was committed to parenting, Mr. Morris had been the girls' primary caregiver because of her demanding work schedule. Within a few months of the divorce, the three-year-old appeared increasingly upset while in her mother's care. She cried at bedtime and called out for her father.

In consultation with a therapist, the parents realized that the toddler was not ready to be away from her father for more than a day at a time. They agreed to adjust the parenting schedule so she spent less time away from her father and also agreed to re-assess their daughter's capacity to tolerate separations in a year.

Chapter Nine

Helping Parents Bridge the Divide with Their Children

When children and their parents drift apart after a divorce, therapists can intervene in different ways. Through individual child therapy, they can help children articulate which family circumstances are upsetting them and help them feel more confident about approaching their parents to discuss their concerns (see chapter 11). Therapists working with divorced parents in individual therapy can help them increase their empathy for their children as one facet of the therapy (see chapter 12). Here, we will focus on how therapists can help divorced parents as an adjunct to individual child therapy or in consultations around parenting that do not include children.

Sometimes therapists are unable to work with divorced parents together because one parent has disappeared from the child's life or does not want to participate, or the parents are unwilling to work together. Below are some of the situations that confront therapists who are working with one parent around a divorce.

REACHING OUT TO ABSENT OR WITHDRAWING PARENTS

When divorce results in the absence or significantly diminished availability of a parent, it often is difficult for therapists to do much to affect that unfortunate circumstance. Freeman et al. (2004) describe the complex process of intervening when a parent has been absent from a child's life for three months of more, noting that the process must address issues of safety and risk, must take heed of the family history (including why the parent withdrew), and must be implemented gradually with careful attention to the child's experience. The authors note that such interventions often are slow and require significant preparatory work.

As described, many parents find the shift to a post-separation visiting arrangement extremely disorienting after sharing a household with their children; some, finding reduced contact too painful to bear, withdraw. Therapists, taking heed of how emotionally painful it is for some parents to have limited contact with children, might suggest a consultation with a divorce expert—perhaps in a mediator role—to review the parenting arrangement and see if some alteration is viable and would serve the children's best interests. Wallerstein and Kelly (1980) found that brief therapeutic interventions with fathers who were struggling with issues around visitation could significantly affect their parental investment in their children. They also found that helping fathers deal with their guilt about leaving can sustain that engagement. In line with Baum's (2004) observation that some fathers' inability to mourn the end of their marriages causes them to withdraw from their children, a referral for individual therapy to help with the mourning process might be appropriate.

ASSISTING PARENTS IN HELPING THEIR CHILDREN MOURN THE LOSS OR ABSENCE OF A PARENT

When one parent has been unable or unwilling to remain in a child's life following a divorce, therapists can assist the remaining parent help the child grieve the loss. Such supported grieving addresses the developmental reality that children need adults' assistance to bear feelings associated with loss. Some parents come for consultations worried about a child's behavior but, because of their own emotional conflicts, are unaware that the child's behavior represents a reaction to loss.

> *Steve, six years old, had been grappling desperately with his father's absence since his parents divorced a year before. His father had called a few times but had forgotten Steve's birthday and had not fulfilled promises to visit. It was clear he was fading out of his son's life. In kindergarten class, Steve wanted to play the baby and pleaded with other children to be his father. He often spoke in baby talk. His teacher responded by setting limits and telling him to act like a big boy. His mother, exasperated, told him he needed to grow up. In response to those failures to understand his suffering, Steve became increasingly withdrawn. At the suggestion of his school, his mother brought him for a consultation.*

In the initial meeting with the therapist, Steve's mother denied that Steve needed help mourning the loss of his father, insisting that he was better off forgetting a man who had proved his unfitness as a parent by absenting himself. The therapist told her that he could understand her perspective but explained that the loss of a parent, even a parent who abandons a child, has huge emotional repercussions and would reverberate for Steve in different ways at different developmental stages. The therapist pointed out that Steve was expressing his grief about his father in his play and his baby talk, dynamics she had difficulty understanding at first because of her fury at Steve's father.

The therapist explained to Steve's mother that her son would need her help acknowledging his loss throughout his childhood and it was urgent that she reach out to help him. He suggested she begin by saying something like: *"I know it is terribly sad for boys when their dads leave after a divorce. I can see that you often miss your dad a great deal. When you feel sad about dad, I would very much like to hear about it so I know what is going on with you. We can think together about what could help you feel better."* In the months that followed, Steve's mother met with the therapist weekly to review her interactions with her son. The therapist helped her refine her comments, which were becoming increasingly sensitive. She was able to voice her despair that she had been left to pick up the pieces after Steve's father went off and started a new life. The therapist expressed admiration of her courage in addressing her ex-husband's decision to withdraw from Steve's life, given how deeply it disturbed her. The therapist also spoke to Steve's teacher to help her, too, understand Steve's emotional turmoil.

Parents like Steve's mother face seemingly contradictory emotional tasks: being steeped in anger as part of disengaging from the former spouse, while simultaneously supporting the child's emotional engagement with that same person (Tessman, 1996). Tessman further observes that children's defensive modes of dealing with loss—often an identification with the missing parent—make it harder for the remaining parent to understand what the child is struggling with, as Steve's mother was unable to do without the therapist's assistance.

Some parents, unlike her, are fully aware that their child is struggling with loss but do not know how to broach the topic.

> *Julie, now four years old, struggled with her feelings about her father's disappearance from her life shortly after her parents' divorce when she was two years old. Julie's mother knew Julie was suffering but brushed off her questions about her father because she felt anguished that Julie had lost him and also feared she would "say the wrong thing." When Julie asked where her father was and what he was doing, her mother responded curtly, "I don't know much, Julie, sorry." Julie, recognizing that her father's absence was a difficult topic for her mother, brought it up less often.*

The therapist encouraged Julie's mother to deal more directly with Julie's questions and create a space for her daughter to express her feelings. When Julie asked where her father was, he suggested her mother say: *"Julie, I don't*

know where your father is. I wish I did. I do know, though, that it is sad and
confusing that he is no longer in touch. Girls so much want to have their
dads in their lives. I wonder what you've been thinking about him." As
Julie's mother began to speak to Julie in this way, Julie began speaking more
openly with her mother about her sadness. The therapist addressed how hard
it was for Julie's mother to acknowledge Julie's sorrow when she herself felt
justifiably angry and disappointed in her ex-husband. He also addressed her
sense of inadequacy in trying to find ways to speak to her daughter, noting
that parents are never taught how to broach difficult topics with their children
and many avoid such topics altogether.

PROVIDING TECHNIQUES FOR ENHANCING
PARENT/CHILD COMMUNICATION

Parents often ask children direct questions: "Are you doing okay with the
divorce?" Children respond with vague or monosyllabic answers: "I'm fine."
Parents sense that their child is *not* okay, but feel befuddled about how to
proceed. In *Growing up with Divorce*, Neil Kalter (1990) demonstrated how
therapists can help parents reach their children by *speaking in displacement*,
a technique well-known to child therapists. In displacement, the parent
speaks about children in general or another child they both know or uses
puppets or dolls to address the difficult issues at hand. Kalter offers detailed
examples of speaking in displacement, tailoring interventions to fit children's
cognitive and emotional capacities. In addition to articulating the child's
emotions and their underlying causes, parents can use displacement to correct the child's misconceptions about the divorce, represent the acceptability
of conflicted feelings, and portray alternative ways of dealing with conflicts.

The technique is especially helpful when parents, like Julie's mother and
Mr. Eaton below, earnestly wish to connect with their children and are open
to feedback.

> *Mr. Eaton expressed exasperation in a parent session that his son, Kyle,*
> *eleven, was unwilling to speak to him about Mr. Eaton's new girlfriend. He*
> *sensed that Kyle was upset. However, when he asked Kyle if he were upset,*
> *Kyle simply said he was "okay." Mr. Eaton was determined to be in close*
> *touch with his son, but felt thwarted.*

The therapist and Mr. Eaton first considered what Kyle might be concerned
about and agreed that he was worried about his father's continued availability
and loyalty conflicts in relation to his mother. The therapist suggested that
Mr. Eaton avoid direct questions, which had led to dead ends, and try saying
the following: *"It's kind of tough on kids when their dads start dating. They*
feel like they're supposed to be happy for their dads, but at the same time

they have all sorts of worries about how life will change. They also feel loyal to their moms and can have a hard time with a new woman coming into the household." The therapist emphasized that Mr. Eaton should not press Kyle to respond to his comment, nor should he follow it up with a direct question. Instead, he should treat it as a "trial balloon"—an idea that is floated out before the child and left to hang there (Neil Kalter, personal communication). If the child does not respond to the trial balloon, that is fine. The parent can try again at a later point.

Therapists can explain to parents that by speaking aloud about their children's worries, they communicate that they understand the child is upset and are prepared to hear about it. At the same time, they avoid pressuring a child to talk, which can contribute to a child's withdrawal. A therapist might explain how, by speaking in displacement, parents respect their child's defenses while still initiating meaningful conversation. As parents work to communicate more effectively with their children, they might jot down brief notes about confusing or troubling interactions with their child and bring them to parent sessions. Concrete examples allow therapists to model specific interventions. Parents learning to speak in displacement often lapse into direct queries that lead their children to shut down. Therapists need to stay patient because parents often find it challenging to speak to their children in what can feel like a foreign language.

ASSISTING A PARENT IN RESPONDING TO CRITICISM FROM THE OTHER PARENT (VIA THE CHILD)

Communication between parents and children often breaks down when children communicate to one parent criticism from the other. As noted, criticized parents tend to become defensive; their natural response is to counter the other parent's assertions.

> *Angela, twelve, returned to her father's home after a weekend with her mother. Her mother had told her she could not go to soccer camp because her father failed to provide the necessary funds. Angela pointedly asked her father why he refused to pay. Mr. Francis, infuriated by what he saw as his ex-wife's distortions, blew up and angrily told Angela that he was not the problem. In fact, her mother was supposed to pay for camps but refused to. Angela yelled at her father that she could never get the truth and stormed out of the room.*

The therapist, working with Angela in individual therapy and meeting with the parents separately, told Mr. Francis he understood he had felt unfairly criticized by his ex-wife (and daughter), which led him to respond to Angela as he had. He told Mr. Francis, though, that his response was not helpful because it led Angela to feel even more caught between her parents. He articulated Angela's bind: trying to navigate relationships with parents who are offering opposite accounts of the same circumstances. The therapist suggested to Mr. Francis that the next time Angela brings a criticism from her mother, he respond by saying: *"I understand it is very confusing for you that your parents, both of whom you love, offer such different versions of the same events. That is so tough. I know that your mother has her view of these events. Not surprisingly, I have a different view. I am sorry you end up feeling so caught and so confused."* Such a response addresses Angela's dilemma and increases the possibility she will feel understood.

I am not suggesting a parent should never defend him- or herself from the other parent's allegations or criticisms. Sometimes, it can be important for parents to share their perspective on a conflicted matter. When they do so, however, it is still helpful if they can acknowledge the child's experience. If Mr. Francis believed it was necessary to clarify the truth about the fees for soccer camp, he might tell Angela: *"I disagree with your mother about the fees for soccer camp. We have an agreement that dictates that she is supposed to pay. But I see why it is confusing to you that we are telling you different things. I guess that's why your mom and I divorced in the first place: We just can't get on the same page."*

While mobilizing a defense in response to the ex-spouse's criticism might help the criticized parent feel better, it is rarely the best approach if a parent hopes to counteract a child's sense of isolation. But because not retaliating runs contrary to a natural impulse to defend ourselves, therapists need to be sensitive to the demands such a non-defensive approach puts on parents and remind them that they are providing a gift to the child by helping him or her disengage from the parents' disagreements and feel understood. At the core of the intervention lies the therapist's effort to bring the child's emotional experience to the foreground for the parent's consideration—an experience that the parent, absorbed in post-divorce tensions, has lost track of.

Parents often argue that the child needs to learn the "reality" of the situation and that in defending themselves they were offering a more accurate perspective. Such lapses in parental empathy can frustrate therapists, who are tuned in to the child's suffering; they can forget how much parents are struggling emotionally and impatiently push them to be more sensitive. It can help therapists if they keep in mind how hard it is to create emotional distance from the ex-spouse after divorce.

HELPING A PARENT RESPOND CONSTRUCTIVELY TO A CHILD'S COMPLAINTS ABOUT THE OTHER PARENT

Some children, especially when they are aware of tensions between the parents, complain to one parent about the other. These are tricky situations for a parent who wishes to support the child's relationship with the other parent but feels concerned about life in the other household.

> *Juan, eleven, was seeing a therapist in individual therapy. The therapist also met with his parents, usually separately. According to Juan's father, Juan often returned to his home complaining that his mother was constantly caught up in doing work on the computer and had recently begun leaving him with a babysitter so she could go out with friends. Juan's father felt angry when he heard Juan's complaint because the behaviors Juan described were consistent with what he viewed as his ex-wife's chronic selfishness. However, he felt unsure what he should say to his son because he was determined not to criticize Juan's mother to Juan. He also wondered how he should respond to Juan's request that he talk with his mother to see if he could "fix the problem."*

The therapist expressed admiration that Juan's father was working so hard to support Juan's relationship with his mother. She also acknowledged the frustration he had to bear because he could not intervene when (at least as Juan presented it) Juan's mother was not attending adequately to him. The therapist suggested that Juan's father encourage Juan to speak directly to his mother about his concerns by reminding his son that these are the sorts of problems that boys need to work out with their mothers. She also suggested that he say to his son: *"I understand that things go on at your mom's house that frustrate you. I am glad you are telling me about them, so I know what is going on with you. Unfortunately, I can't really talk to your mom about these problems because, as you know, we get too tense and start arguing. That's too bad and it makes your life harder, but it's part of the divorce. That's why you are going to have to work this out with her yourself."* Such a statement seeks to promote father/son communication, keep Juan out of the middle, and also counteract Juan's apparent denial of the fact that his parents are unable to work well together.

HELPING PARENTS ADDRESS THEIR CHILDREN'S "BETWEEN-TWO-WORLDS" EXPERIENCE

The interventions described immediately above—helping parents respond thoughtfully to ex-spouses' criticisms and to children's complaints about the other parent—are important in part because they address the reality that these children have to navigate lives in two households divided by tensions and divergent approaches to daily life. By explicitly acknowledging the associated challenges, parents can ameliorate children's feelings of aloneness.

Divorced parents often describe miserable transitions between households—how it takes a day or two to get their children back to normal after their return. Frustrated by unpleasant interactions that detract from precious parenting time, parents often blame the other parent or express open disappointment in the child's behavior. Therapists can help parents understand the challenges of living in two households and find language to address them.

> *Martin, ten, struggled to adjust to his parents' alternating-week parenting arrangement. Following each transition, he was angry and distant for a day or two before he finally settled down. His parents had been asking him what was going on to no avail and finally had set strict limits on his behaviors.*

The therapist suggested that after Martin arrived back at his or her home, each parent tell him something like: *"I can see you are having a tough time leaving your mom's/dad's house to come to my house. I can imagine it is tough to say goodbye to your mom/dad and have to adjust to life in a different house. I get the sense that you feel pretty stressed out when you make the move. A lot of boys get angry and withdrawn when they feel sad and stressed. I am wondering what I can do to help you feel less stressed out."* The therapist supported the parents in setting limits on Martin when he misbehaved. However, he emphasized that Martin would, importantly, feel understood if his parents saw his acting-out behaviors as a response to stress rather than his simply being the "brat" his father accused him of being.

Script [handwritten annotation in left margin with bracket]

Pedro-Carroll (2010) offers useful recommendations for reducing children's stress level around transitions. She recommends that parents live as close together as possible. In addition, children should know the schedule, which will increase their sense of security. Parents should provide their children with "positive preparation" (p. 160) by encouraging their enthusiasm for time spent with the other parent. Allowing children to have special belongings at both homes and to be able to bring belongings back and forth also helps. She also recommends that parents allow children easy access to the other parent through phone calls, texting, and email.

HELPING PARENTS BEAR THEIR CHILDREN'S DISAPPOINTMENT

As noted, children rarely broach the topic of their disappointment in their parents directly or constructively. When they do try, parents are likely to rebuff them.

> *Twelve-year-old Becky feels intensely disappointed in her mother whom she blames, angrily, for her parents' divorce when she was ten. She misses having her father in the house and expresses outrage that her parents could not work out their differences. In the face of Becky's verbal attacks, Ms. Greenberg defends herself by asserting that she had no choice; she had to leave Mr. Greenberg so she could get on with her life. Becky persists, insisting that both parents are selfish. Finally, fed up, Ms. Greenberg explodes, accusing Becky*

of being selfish and failing to appreciate her mother's unhappiness in the
marriage. She tells Becky to "shut up" if she cannot find something nice to
say.

Becky's therapist tells Ms. Greenberg he can appreciate that she felt hurt by
her daughter's comments and that, feeling hurt, she became angry. (Implicit-
ly here he is interested in helping Ms. Greenberg understand how her own
anger blocks out awareness of her hurt feelings, so that she might in turn
understand Becky's outbursts.) At the same time, he suggests that Becky is
expressing expectable disappointment, even if she does not do it in a helpful
or mature way. He reminds Ms. Greenberg that while she may have had
excellent reasons for divorcing, she and Becky's father still subjected Becky
to heartache.

The therapist recommends that Ms. Greenberg say to her daughter: *"I
understand you are really disappointed in me. I made a decision that has*
affected your life a great deal and did not include you. You wanted your
father and me to stay together. We tried very hard to work it out but we failed
you because we were unable." By addressing the hard reality of the family
situation and speaking to the disappointment underlying Becky's anger, Ms.
Greenberg's words seek to counteract Becky's need to stay immersed in
anger. By providing those words to Ms. Greenberg, the therapist tries to help
her separate her own experience of the divorce from Becky's.

While it is helpful for parents to acknowledge that a child is disappointed
and to take responsibility for a divorce, parents must not allow the child to
use this acknowledgment to justify abusive behaviors. Optimally, parents
would make clear that they are willing to hear about the child's unhappiness
but are unwilling to be spoken to disrespectfully. Therapists can help parents
set parameters: *"I am open to hearing about your unhappiness about the*
divorce. In fact, I genuinely want to know how you feel. At the same time, I
am unwilling to serve as your punching bag. You need to stay respectful and
speak to me appropriately. If you start calling me names, the conversation
will end."

As parents set limits on angry behaviors successfully, they will need to
help their children deal with the feelings that these behaviors masked.

> *Jack, six, exploded angrily at his mother each time his father failed to show up*
> *for scheduled visits. Sometimes, enraged, he hit her. Jack's therapist worked*
> *with Jack's mother to set clear limits on Jack's outbursts and to restrain him*
> *firmly when he escalated in his behaviors. They discussed how, when Jack was*
> *calmer, she could speak to him about his disappointment that his father, once*
> *again, had failed to show up. She began to say to her son: "Boys feel so*
> *disappointed and sad when their dads do not come to visit. And when they feel*
> *sad, they often get real mad because it is so hard to feel so sad."*

As Jack began to recognize how upset he was about his father's absences, he began to settle down. His mother then began to work with Jack to anticipate how he might feel if his father did not show up at the appointed time, increasing his sense of mastery over his difficult feelings.

Mothers and sons often run into trouble post-divorce because boys are furious and mothers, worn out by economic strain, work, and other demands (and sometimes accustomed to having had the father function as disciplinarian), have trouble managing their sons' rage. In such situations, a parent might require concrete guidance for discipline: when to insist that behaviors are unacceptable and how to impose consequences in the face of misbehavior. Hetherington and Kelly (2002) found that behavior modification programs for parents were especially helpful for newly divorced mothers, who learned how to discipline their children more effectively and became less susceptible to their children's coercive behaviors. When parents continue to have trouble implementing suggestions for limit-setting, therapists should consider that parents' guilt over the divorce is impeding their capacity to step in more decisively. In such situations, a child therapist might refer a parent for individual therapy.

INTERVENING WHEN ONE PARENT IS DENIGRATING THE OTHER

Working with parents who are denigrating the other parent to the children is an especially challenging task because such people have lost track of the child's experience. The therapist has to figure out how to help them engage or re-engage their empathy.

> *Carlos, eleven, voiced a wish to live with his father after having lived primarily with his mother for the first four years after the divorce. In the initial consultation for therapy, Carlos described how his mother badmouthed his father and his father's family, which Carlos found unbearable. In a joint session with Carlos, his mother, Ms. Havens, spoke angrily about Carlos's inability to see that his father was too immature to function as a full-time parent. She kept hammering home her points. Caught up in making her case, she failed to recognize that her words were wounding her son.*

The therapist learned that Ms. Havens believed many extended family members idealized her ex-husband and, in doing so, glossed over his lapses as a father that had made her life hard over the years, including his lack of financial responsibility. Children, especially boys, often idealize non-custodial fathers, even when they have assumed much less parental responsibility post-divorce than mothers. Such idealization is a source of torment for many weary mothers.

The therapist quickly understood that he could not help Ms. Havens become more sensitive to Carlos if she felt that the therapist failed to understand her perceptions of her ex-husband. Determined to maintain a positive relationship with both parents, though, the therapist was careful not to simply agree with her assertion that her husband was "an irresponsible slob." Instead, he acknowledged that she experienced him that way. Baris et al. (2001) suggest that this type of intervention with an angry parent demands artistry: Clinicians need to demonstrate that while they understand the parent's perception of the other parent, they see the situation differently, and they need to do so without making it sound like a challenge to the parent's defenses.

The therapist worked to help Ms. Havens recognize that her efforts to press Carlos to agree with her views of his father were backfiring, leading her son to feel more alienated from her and more allied with his father. A therapist, by empathizing with the denigrating parent's distress, can begin to create an alliance that allows him or her to bring the child's emotional experience to the parent's attention. In that role, the therapist might say to Ms. Havens: *"I recognize how hard it is for you that Carlos does not seem to see the negative features of his father that you find so frustrating. From Carlos's perspective, though, he has one father and, understandably, wants to admire him. Your criticisms feel to him as if you were taking something special away from him. They also make him feel as if he has to choose between you and his father, which is intolerable because he loves you both."* [Script]

This sort of intervention may need to be repeated in different ways at different times. The therapist has to be steadfast and patient and recognize that the denigrating parent's need to put the other parent down, however distasteful, originates in deep feelings of hurt and betrayal and will not be given up easily. Therapists need to be careful that, in identification with the child's suffering, they do not become overzealous, impatient or hectoring toward the parent or they will rapidly lose therapeutic leverage.

For a parent like Ms. Havens, troubled by her son's idealization of his father, it can be reassuring if the therapist explains that developing more realistic perceptions of a parent is a critical developmental task of childhood, especially adolescence, and that Carlos is likely to recognize his father's limitations over time. The therapist can emphasize that children have to manage this developmental task on their own time line, recognizing the disappointing aspects of a parent as they become emotionally ready to do so. The therapist might explain to Ms. Havens that if she presses Carlos to see things about his father before he is ready, she is taking him outside his emotional comfort zone.

It also can be helpful to explain to a denigrating parent that children develop a sense of self based in part on identifications with *both* parents. Therefore, a parent's proffering a diminished view of the other parent adversely affects a child's self-esteem. Sometimes, awareness of how down-grading the other parent can affect a child's self-esteem is enough to get a parent to recognize the damage she or he is inflicting and stop. When that approach is inadequate, the therapist might try to help a parent understand the bind he or she is creating by forcing the child to choose one parent.

If a child complains that a parent's harsh comments about the other parent are upsetting, the therapist might ask the child for permission to talk with the parent about this matter. Here, privacy between therapist and child becomes less important than finding a way to address an untenable external stressor. In my experience, children usually are open to therapists talking to parents about such matters because they are desperate for help. Alternatively, a therapist might invite the parent to meet together with the child to see if the child, with some support, can explain to the parent how difficult she or he finds the parent's behavior. Finally, a therapist might work in individual therapy with a child to help him or her find ways to speak to a parent more assertively.

REFERRING

If it becomes clear that the child's suffering is caused mainly by a parent's mental health problems (e.g., a reactive depression in response to the divorce), the therapist may have limited options for intervening with the parent, especially if the parent is already getting help from another therapist. If a parent is not getting help, the therapist might suggest that the parent do so and initiate a referral. It is important in referring a parent in a divorce situation that the referred-to therapist be sensitive to the dynamics of divorce and not simply ally with the parent against the opposite parent, as some therapists, unfortunately, are wont to do. If parents resist a referral, the child's therapist can use knowledge of the child to nudge parents gently. For instance, if the therapist determines that a parent's anxiety is burdening a child, the therapist can use that information as leverage to help the parent see that a consultation for personal therapy is important for the *child's* well-being.

HELPING PARENTS ASSIST THEIR CHILDREN IN ADAPTING TO NEW PARTNERS

Parents' engagement with new partners, whether brief affairs or remarriage, often strain their relationships with their children, as noted. Therapists can help by educating parents about what their children find hard in these circumstances. I advise divorced parents to tilt in the direction of being conservative about introducing children to new lovers and to anticipate their children's reluctance to connect. The therapist functions to keep children's experience front and center: for instance, how hard it is for children to attach to a new adult when they anticipate anxiously that the relationship will end as their parents' did. Therapists might also advocate a conservative approach to exposing the child to the parent's sexuality, helping parents understand that children can feel overstimulated by a too-early confrontation with their parents' sexual relationships. The therapist speaks to the hidden emotional experiences children are unable to express in words but express instead through withdrawal or angry acting out.

> *Ms. Issa, recently divorced, learned to her dismay that her son had learned from a classmate (who had seen the couple at a movie) that Ms. Issa had a new boyfriend. When her son confronted her angrily and wanted to know if she was sleeping with the boyfriend. Ms. Issa, anxious, avoided the question until she spoke to her therapist. The therapist said it was very important for her to explain to her son that she was open to talking about lots of things, but certain parts of her life needed to be private. The therapist suggested she also say something about how confusing it must be for her son to imagine her spending time with a man other than his father.*

Parents and stepparents often need assistance around issues of discipline because, as noted, when stepparents step in quickly in a disciplinary role, they can alienate children, who tend to question their legitimacy. Usually it is best for the biological parent to function as disciplinarian. The stepparent can assist by offering suggestions and support. I often make the analogy of the coach sending in plays from the sideline to the quarterback, who is caught up in the fray and appreciates the wisdom of the more dispassionate onlooker. (This analogy does not mean to imply that the coach is wiser, just a step removed from the action.)

Parents who remarry often need help understanding that children need time to develop a relationship with a new parenting figure (Hodges, 1991). Otherwise, the stepparent and child can lose a rich opportunity for building a close relationship. Therapists might need to explain the reasons a child does not share the parent's excitement: a struggle with a loyalty conflict in relation to the biological parent, for instance, or a confrontation with the stark reality that the parents will not be getting back together due to remarriage.

> *Two years after her divorce, Ms. Johnson fell in love with a man and decided to remarry. While her sons, ten and eleven, and her daughter, fourteen, expressed pleasure about her decision and reassured their mother that they were delighted at her choice, they were more withdrawn and less spontaneous at home. Ms. Johnson sensed that they were upset about the pending changes in their lives, but felt unsure about how to talk with them. She wondered if bringing up the topic of her marriage would upset them more. She asked a therapist for guidance.*

The therapist asked Ms. Johnson to provide details about her children's remarks about her decision to marry. From her account, he understood that
they had enjoyed having their mother to themselves after the divorce and, as
she became increasingly involved with a new man, they became upset about
her diminished availability and worried about the future. The therapist
worked to help Ms. Johnson increase her awareness of her children's anxiety,
explaining how jarring the change must feel for them, despite their protestations to the contrary. It is important to note here that the therapist needed to
help Ms. Johnson understand her children's defenses: how the simultaneous
combination of reassurance and withdrawal reflected their efforts to manage
feelings they found difficult to speak about directly.

The therapist suggested to Ms. Johnson that she say to her children: *"I
appreciate that you are happy for me about my decision to marry, but I can't
imagine it is all peaches and cream. I get the sense sometimes that you worry
about how the marriage will affect our relationship, even though you do not
say it directly."* The therapist worked with Ms. Johnson to address her un-
ease about her children's anxiety, reassuring her that she and they could find
constructive ways to deal with the changes in their lives, especially if she
found a way to talk more openly. It became clear, as is often the case with
divorcing parents, that Ms. Johnson felt guilty about their anxieties and
found it upsetting to learn more about them, even though, simultaneously,
she wanted to be in close contact with her children.

COUNTERTRANSFERENCE CHALLENGES

Some child and adolescent therapists take special pleasure in the idea of
establishing the most intimate child/adult relationship their child or adolescent patients have. In unconscious competition with the children's parents—
often linked to therapists' wishes to be superior to their own parents—they
privilege their relationships with their child patients over their child patients'
relationships with their parents by focusing almost exclusively on individual
therapy and relegating parents to the periphery. In doing so, they forget that
children's healthy development rests in considerable part on their ability to
work out a close relationship with their parents, who are with the child day in
and day out and will be part of the children's lives long after the therapist is
gone.

Frustrating features of parent work also can contribute to some therapists'
tendency to keep parents at the periphery. Therapists often find that, despite
their best efforts, parents stay stuck. For instance, they pepper a child with
direct questions instead of speaking in displacement or attack a child for
being selfish instead of inviting a dialogue about the child's disappointment.
In such situations, the therapist has a subtle diagnostic assessment to make: Is

the parent failing to understand the suggestions and needing more repetition and practice? Is the parent being passive-aggressive, subtly undermining the therapist's suggestions out of hostility or skepticism? Or, is the parent too upset to deal with the child's suffering? Each of these possibilities would dictate a different sort of intervention.

We as therapists do the work we do, at least in part, because it is important for us to help people who are suffering. The reasons it is important often run very deep into our own childhoods. When suffering people thwart our best efforts to influence them, we feel frustrated, even sad and inadequate. Working with divorcing parents can challenge the steadfastness of even the most dedicated therapists because the forces that interfere with their empathy for their children are often deep-seated and, at times, refractory to intervention. We as therapists need to monitor ourselves. When we feel angry and critical, we might consider using the same exercise we might suggest to angry parents and children: examine the feelings that underlie the anger. Are we feeling helpless? Inadequate? Closed out? Are these familiar feelings that have a long history? Do they tell us something important about how stuck the family is feeling?

In working with families of divorce, especially those mired in conflict, it is important to be aware of our expectations so we can consider how realistic they are. We may be burning out because we think we should be able to exert more influence than, in fact, we reasonably can. While therapeutic optimism is critical to staying engaged over time, overzealousness becomes a trap when it does not allow us to adjust to situations in which progress moves at a snail's pace (or not at all). Sometimes, therapists deny the extent of a family's psychological disturbance, especially when parents have personality disorders or major mental illness. Severe psychological disturbance is always troubling to confront, even for experienced clinicians, especially when it is damaging children.

Chapter Ten

Working with Parents in the High-Conflict Divorce

While high-conflict divorces occur with relative infrequency, as noted, most clinicians will confront such divorces at some point. They might work in therapy with a child being buffeted by parents' feuding, for instance, or a furious parent in the midst of a bitter breakup. Understanding these divorces, especially how they affect therapists emotionally, is critical to knowing how to deal with them. High-conflict divorces are more volatile and inflammatory than more ordinary divorces, but their *dynamics* are the same—two people struggling emotionally to disengage from a (presumably) close relationship. Therefore, though exhausting and depleting to work with, high-conflict divorces are illuminating because they expose clinicians in a crystallized, vivid way to interpersonal forces they will encounter in *all* divorces.

THERAPISTS CAUGHT IN THE STORM
CREATED BY PARENTS' CONFLICT

Dr. D., an experienced psychologist, was asked by divorced parents to provide therapy to their young adolescent son following a highly contentious divorce. Because the parents refused to meet together, Dr. D. met with them separately. Ms. Nance described Mr. Nance as an aloof, obsessive accountant who was so absorbed in computer games that he did not attend to their son. She conveyed that her observations about Mr. Nance were obvious; she was certain Dr. D. would agree when he met him.

Dr. D. found himself caught up in Ms. Nance's account of her ex-husband and expected upon meeting him that he, too, would be concerned about this man's impact on his son. However, Mr. Nance threw him a curveball. An awkward, shy man, more comfortable with numbers than people, Mr. Nance nonetheless had a genuine investment in parenting his son. He described activ-

113

*ities they enjoyed together—he was teaching him computer programming—
and showed a surprising attunement to his son's likes and dislikes.*

In order to work effectively with children and adolescents in a high-conflict
divorce, therapists must be able to carve out a space between the feuding
parents and serve as a neutral consultant to the family whose focus is the
children's needs. Unless therapists maintain a positive relationship with each
parent, they run the risk of contributing to already damaging polarization.
However, because these parents urgently need others to fortify their fragile
defenses, they insist that therapists (like others around them) ally with their
black-and-white visions of reality, making it extremely difficult for therapists
to find a neutral place to stand. In contrast to the majority of divorcing
parents whose desire for guidance is genuine and who are at least reasonably
amenable to feedback, feuding parents like Ms. Nance and Mr. Nance tend to
seek confirmation of their views on the bad behaviors/character of the ex-
spouse and vindication of their own behaviors/character. Therapists, in order
to form alliances with their patients, work hard to find ways to experience
them as likeable, even when they are difficult to deal with. The formidable
pressures that high-conflict parents place on therapists dovetail with therapists' natural tendencies to ally with their patients' perspectives, increasing
the pull on therapists to move toward one parent or the other.

Individuals mired in high conflict indicate that their views regarding the
ex-spouse are obvious and that anybody with sense—much less a therapist
with presumed diagnostic acumen—will see the situation as they do. Therapists discern immediately, though not always consciously, that parents who
create simplistic views of complex family circumstances are under enormous
internal pressure, desperately erecting barriers against being flooded by their
underlying feelings, like a person frantically stacking sand bags to protect a
home from onrushing water. Therapists want to help and, like anybody in the
helping professions, want people to appreciate their skills, including their
capacity to empathize with a suffering person. They become aware, though,
that they will face a parent's disdain, if not outright rage, if they do not
accept that parent's views of the divorce, including the harsh assessment of
the ex-spouse. They will be labeled insensitive or inadequate—one more on a
list of hurtful people in the parent's life.

Dr. D. anticipated that Ms. Nance would become agitated if he questioned
her perceptions, even if he tread gingerly. She might accuse him of failing to
see the obvious or, worse, of failing to protect her son, a weighty accusation
for a clinician devoted to children's care. Dr. D. anticipated his second interview with Ms. Nance with quiet dread. Under these sorts of emotional pressures, therapists are vulnerable to aligning with a person's defensively driven
views of the family situation rather than bearing the discomfort of calling
those views into question (Ehrlich, 2001). While therapists might alienate a

parent if they challenge his or her perspective, they make matters worse if they ally unilaterally with that parent's views because doing so provides support for a distorted view of the family situation and precludes the opportunity to speak to underlying feelings the parent is fending off and, optimally, help move him or her toward mourning.

In advance of his coming session with Ms. Nance, Dr. D. prepared himself emotionally in an effort to stay neutral. He reminded himself that Ms. Nance felt bereft as a result of the divorce and that her outrage emanated from hurt feelings. During the parent session, Dr. D. began by telling Ms. Nance that he appreciated her concerns about her ex-husband's parenting. In an effort to address her narcissistic vulnerability, he applauded her devotion to parenting and noted the particular strengths she had that benefitted their son. At the same time, he told Ms. Nance that he could see qualities in her ex-husband that might serve their son well, however exasperating they were to her, and he worked to distinguish Ms. Nance's experience of Mr. Nance from her son's experience of his father, noting that the very qualities she found so frustrating (e.g., his absorption in computer games), her son appreciated. In an effort to bring her son's needs to the forefront, Dr. D. reminded Ms. Nance that her son had one father and that his working out the best relationship possible with his father would serve his developmental needs.

THERAPIST MISSTEPS IN THE HIGH-CONFLICT DIVORCE

Dr. D., experienced with high-conflict divorces and aware of Ms. Nance's vulnerability, was able to carve out a space between the parents that allowed him to begin to intervene effectively. However, when therapists fail to recognize parents' severe narcissistic disturbances, they are unlikely to comprehend that these parents' descriptions of the family situation, including those of the ex-spouse, reflect an urgent effort to establish narcissistic equilibrium, not a well-reasoned account. The probability of therapists gaining a skewed perspective increases dramatically when they work with one parent in individual therapy or see a child in therapy that includes only one parent and so lack access to the divergent perspectives at play. Visions of rescuing a child or adult also draw therapists unwittingly into complex high-conflict divorce dramas (Johnston and Campbell, 1988). Because adults caught up in feuds present clear, convincing accounts, even experienced therapists can lose their bearings and assume they understand more about what is going on than they actually do. In the face of such pushes and pulls, therapists are highly vulnerable to exacerbating family tensions and even committing ethical violations.

Ms. W., a tough-minded attorney/mediator, was progressing in her work with the O'Brien parents and was pleased she was able to get them to agree to Mr. O'Brien's idea of arranging a psychiatric consultation for their adolescent son, who was depressed and possibly suicidal. But Ms. W. was stunned when Ms. O'Brien stormed into the next mediation session and asserted she no longer supported a psychiatric consultation. Ms. O'Brien announced that her therapist had advised her that she was being bullied by her ex-husband and urged her to put her foot down.

Ms. W. was perplexed that Ms. O'Brien's therapist had so profoundly misunderstood the circumstances, especially because she had worked to ensure that Ms. O'Brien's voice was heard during mediation. Because she believed the adolescent needed a psychiatric evaluation, Ms. W. viewed Mr. O'Brien's request as appropriate, not as a maneuver to gain more power. She wondered why, if the therapist were so concerned, he had not gotten a consent to speak to her so they could discuss the family situation. Ms. O'Brien's therapist likely saw himself as a passionate advocate on behalf of his besieged patient and apparently never considered that Ms. O'Brien might be presenting a slanted version of what was going on in the mediation and was *using* the therapist to buttress her defenses. Ms. O'Brien's therapist, by exacerbating Ms. O'Brien's righteous outrage at her husband, contributed to an escalation of the parents' tensions and failed to help his patient come to terms with the end of the marriage.

When divorcing parents present persuasive accounts in support of their own views, therapists can easily be swept into overestimating their accuracy and thereby underestimating the psychopathology underlying them (Wallerstein, 1990). The result can be a damaging misapprehension of the family circumstances.

Mr. Perez, seeking an ally in his custody battle over his eleven-year-old son, arranged a consultation with a local psychiatrist. An articulate, forceful man, Mr. Perez explained in compelling detail how his wife displayed the symptoms of a severe borderline personality disorder and was enmeshed dangerously with their son. The psychiatrist, alarmed by Mr. Perez's description and eager to help, wrote a letter to the court supporting Mr. Perez's contention that he should have full custody.

The psychiatrist, by blindly siding with Mr. Perez's views without gathering adequate data, manifested clinical and ethical lapses that are common in highly conflicted divorces. Having the psychiatrist as his ally bolstered Mr. Perez's defensively driven retaliatory stance and supported the righteousness of his quest for custody. The psychiatrist committed an ethical lapse by making recommendations about custody without having conducted a full evaluation (which would involve both parents, the children, and the court's imprimatur).

In the context of high-conflict divorces, mental health professionals are surprisingly prone to making such formulations about parents they have never met. The egregiousness of such lapses correlates with the forcefulness of the pull that feuding parents exert and therapists' ignorance of these parents' impact. When confronted about her role, the psychiatrist became defensive. She asserted that she had ample data to make the diagnosis she did, arguing that she was ethically obligated to protect the children from their disturbed mother. She was so swayed by Mr. Perez's account that she was unable to consider that the family situation was far more complicated than Mr. Perez indicated.

CHALLENGES TO STAYING CALM, KIND AND ENGAGED

The Groundhog Day Experience

In working with narcissistically vulnerable parents, it behooves therapists to be gentle, patient, and non-judgmental and to focus on their strengths be-cause these parents need help saving face (Johnston and Campbell, 1988), especially when they have felt shamed by a spouse who rejected them. These parents can be galling and exasperating, however, when they remain volatile and unamenable to reason. Dealing with parents who are unable to mourn and move on with their lives is like going through Bill Murray's nightmarish experience in *Groundhog Day*—waking up and finding that every day is exactly the same. No matter how patient therapists might be, none of us likes to be shut down exactly as we were on previous occasions when we offer what we believe to be well-conceived suggestions.

Therapeutic zeal is especially problematic with the high-conflict divorce because these situations, by definition, tend to resist intervention. Therapists have to manage frustration and tedium (Johnston, Roseby, and Kuehnle, 2009) in persisting with painstaking work and bear feeling helpless and inad-equate as they grapple with situations that can foil their best efforts at help-ing. Therapists must seek what can feel like an impossible balance between, on the one hand, persisting in the face of very gradual progress or none at all, and, on the other hand, recognizing the limits of interventions so they do not burn out (and withdraw or retaliate against the parents). It can be helpful to think about *managing* symptoms in the high-conflict divorce, not curing or erasing them (Baris et al., 2001).

Managing Frustration and Irritation

The imperviousness of high-conflict parents to their children's emotional needs is further disturbing to therapists, who almost reflexively identify with distressed children. Wallerstein (1990) believes that the dramatic deteriora-tion of these parents' relationships with their children around divorce elicits in clinicians "a combination of anguish and impotent rage" (p. 340). Because their emotional reactions inevitably affect their interactions with parents, they might find themselves withdrawing, then rationalizing their withdrawal without being fully aware of the reasons.

> *Dr. C. was treating Brian, twelve, in weekly therapy that focused on helping him cope with his parents' incessant bickering. Dr. C. understood he needed to include Brian's parents in the therapy to try to help them settle down (or, if not, perhaps refer them to a co-parenting therapist). After seeing the parents a few times, however, Dr. C. found himself avoiding them, which he initially attributed to logistical challenges with scheduling appointments. On reflection, though, he realized he simply could not stand sitting in a room with these people as they locked horns once again.*

Therapists, exasperated by the stuck quality of high-conflict parents, run the risk of becoming judgmental with parents who are least able to manage it emotionally. It can help therapists stay patient and kind if they keep in mind that these parents implement their defenses, no matter how destructive, because they *need* them psychically to manage separation and loss. Schafer (1983) reminds us of the imperative, in working with people's defenses, to proceed carefully, patiently, and with full empathic awareness of the person's underlying fears. Keeping in mind the often traumatic histories of high-conflict parents also helps (Johnston, Roseby, and Kuehnle, 2009). Maintaining empathy can be extraordinarily difficult when, for example, we see a parent harming a child, but confronting parents with their destructiveness, however tempting and maybe even helpful on occasion, runs the risk of alienating them and foreclosing intervention.

> *Mr. B. became increasingly impatient with Ms. Quigley, the mother of seven-year-old Darlene, whom Mr. B. was seeing in individual therapy. During every parenting session, when Mr. B. tried to help Ms. Quigley understand Darlene's distress, she shifted the focus from Darlene to how Darlene's father was driving her up a wall by badgering her. A few times, Mr. B. snapped at Ms. Quigley to focus on Darlene, not her ex-husband.*

Mr. B. understood that the content of what she said may have been reasonable and even helpful, but he let his frustration with Ms. Quigley infiltrate his intervention in a way that made it impossible for her to absorb. Mr. B. had to work hard to repair the damage he caused in their relationship

Feeling Misused and Diminished

Parents in difficult divorces, especially those who have felt rejected by their spouses, often maintain fervent hopes that therapists will, in addition to bolstering their defenses, fulfill selfobject functions they desperately need in order to feel better about themselves—will offer admiration and also provide someone they can idealize. But when parents use therapists primarily as selfobjects, they tend to devalue their expertise—the unique characteristics such as refined empathy and specialized training that make therapists feel special and competent—so that therapists can feel as if they are not being seen or valued. If (or, perhaps more accurately, when) a therapist disappoints a parent or manifests a lapse in empathy, the parent can shift quickly from idealization to devaluation and accusation.

> *Dr. T. enjoyed his reputation as battle-hardened wizard with high-conflict divorces. He felt flattered when Ms. Randolph told him she heard he could "work miracles." He felt increasingly anxious, however, when Ms. Randolph began to express disappointment that progress toward helping her and her ex-husband co-parent more effectively was slow. He felt even more uneasy when he learned that Ms. Randolph had complained to her attorney about the slow progress, especially because Ms. Randolph's attorney, who idealized Dr. T., was a source of frequent referrals.*

Therapists have to tolerate feeling misused, dismissed, and diminished in order to stay fully engaged with feuding parents. To do so, they must become aware of *their own* narcissistic struggles that bear on their work—wishes to be admired, successful, brilliantly imaginative (Wilson, 2004; Chused, 2012). Such wishes, alive in all therapists, come to the fore with intensity with patients who idealize then quickly devalue them.

Therapists can find it disturbing to become the repository of parents' projections in high-conflict divorces (Johnston, Roseby, and Kuehnle, 2009). They suggest that therapists need to consider their own reactions carefully before intervening therapeutically. My own clinical work confirms that the first task for therapists is allowing themselves to become as aware as possible of how they are thinking and feeling and to view their emotional reactions as meaningful.

> *Dr. K., an experienced child psychologist, worked hard to carve out a middle space between Ms. Short and her husband as he worked with them on co-parenting their children more effectively. Ms. Short recently had learned about Mr. Short's affair with his secretary and was angry and depressed. Dr. K. empathized with Ms. Short's outrage over her husband's affair and tried to be as gentle with her as possible. No matter what he said, however, Ms. Short spoke to him in quiet fury.*
>
> *Dr. K. found himself feeling guilty, as if he himself had harmed Ms. Short. He began to withdraw from offering his ideas out of fear that he would offend her further. On reflection, Dr. K. realized that he had come to feel in the parent sessions that he was one more "asshole" man who did not care about women and that Ms. Short was right to be disgusted with him.*

Dr. K., caught in Ms. Short's projections, struggled to maintain an image of himself as a decent, caring man who was genuinely trying to help this family. As he recognized upon reflection that he had not, in fact, been unkind to Ms. Short—that she was attributing to him feelings she had about all men at that moment—he was able to mobilize himself to intervene more energetically. He let Ms. Short know that she needed to find a way to work with her husband, despite her understandable outrage. Therapists, especially those who lack experience with the high-conflict divorce, are vulnerable to these parents' accusations of insensitivity and to believing they actually *were* unkind or non-empathic, as opposed to recognizing that it is almost impossible to question the views of a parent in a high-conflict divorce without provoking fierce backlash.

After becoming aware of their strong reactions to high-conflict parents, therapists have to bear and metabolize feelings these parents cannot tolerate within themselves. Often this requires honest scrutiny of one's own strong feelings.

> *Ms. C., a family therapist, found herself feeling protective of Mr. Thatcher, whose wife's affair left him bereft and crushed. Ms. Thatcher appeared oblivious to the impact of her affair on her husband. To Ms. C.'s dismay, Ms. Thatcher accused her husband of overreacting, opining that he needed to get over it. After all it had been three months since he first learned of the affair.*

Ms. Thatcher, unable to bear her guilt over hurting her husband so badly, disavowed feelings of concern for a man to whom she had been married for twenty years by effecting a distant, critical stance. Ms. C. became the repository of a protective concern for Mr. Thatcher that Ms. Thatcher herself was unable to tolerate. Ms. C. fantasized about shaking Ms. Thatcher by the lapels and shouting at her: How can you be so cruel to a man you once loved? Can you not see that he is devastated? Aware of these urges, however, Ms. C. worked them over in her mind in anticipation of her next interview with Ms. Thatcher. Feeling calmer, she was able to suggest gently that getting over a spouse's affair often takes longer than three months. She said she could imagine that Ms. Thatcher, a thoughtful person, could understand that. Ms. Thatcher softened and said, yes, she could.

SOME KEYS TO AVOIDING MISSTEPS IN WORKING WITH THE HIGH-CONFLICT DIVORCE

Recognizing the High-Conflict Divorce as Early as Possible

Because therapists can easily be pulled into clinical and ethical missteps in working with a high-conflict divorce, their first task is recognizing as early as possible the situation they are dealing with. Protracted litigation usually indicates a high-conflict divorce. In addition, if a parent presents a unidimensional account with a highly critical description of the other parent, that should be a warning to clinicians to take heed. Baris et al. (2001) offer a Conflict Assessment Scale that can help therapists to identify a high-conflict divorce early. It categorizes conflict as either minimal, mild, moderate, moderately severe, and severe, and provides specific criteria for assessment. The authors also offer criteria for assessing the degree of narcissistic disturbance in parents based on the degree of their narcissistic vulnerability, the concomitant defenses, and their behavioral manifestations in relation to the children and the spouse.

Chethik et al. (1984), approaching parents from a psychoanalytic perspective, suggest that clinicians working with divorced parents must clarify the parents' level of narcissistic disturbance before they can know how to pitch interventions. They differentiate among transitory narcissistic stress, narcissistic regression, and severe narcissistic vulnerability (exacerbated by the divorce). They offer criteria to clarify levels of disturbance, including the quality of the parent/child relationship prior to the divorce, the capacity for self-observation, and the pervasiveness of narcissistic conflicts. The authors assert that intensive individual interventions are needed for the most narcissistically vulnerable parents, some of whom will not be amenable to intervention at all, however. Johnston and Campbell (1988) similarly distinguish among mild, moderate, and severe narcissistic disturbance and delineate differential interventions appropriate to the severity of the narcissistic disturbance.

Bearing Ambiguity Long Enough to Know how to Intervene

While therapists ordinarily have to bear ambiguity in their daily work, they are not usually forced to question their patients' versions of reality (unless, perhaps, they are working with severely traumatized or psychotic patients). In the high-conflict divorce, though, when parents present divergent—even diametrically opposed—versions of the same circumstances, therapists can feel beset by mind-numbing uncertainty and confusion.

> *Ms. L., an experienced child therapist, met separately with the parents of Nathan, an eleven-year-old boy whose parents recently divorced and who was acting out in school. Nathan's mother told Ms. L. that Nathan was reacting to his father's extramarital affairs. However, his father vehemently denied any infidelity and told Ms. L. that Nathan's mother had had an affair with the local tennis coach that was the talk of the neighborhood and was leading other children to tease Nathan.*

Different versions of reality cannot both be fully accurate, though each may contain accurate elements, which make them extremely hard to sort out. A man might describe his sad ex-wife as severely depressed. A woman might describe her absent-minded ex-husband as dangerously self-absorbed. A parent who had a lively email correspondence with a high school flame reportedly had a torrid affair. When parents present their tilted stories with absolute certainty and confirmatory data, therapists can feel fully convinced by one parent's version of events and then, a day later, fully convinced by the other parent that the first parent was distorting. Further information from the first parent will call the second parent's account into question and so on. Staying calm in the face of such ambiguity is hard, especially when a parent raises concerns about children's safety. Therapists can feel as if they were losing their ordinary intellectual capacities to order the world around them.

Ms. L., perplexed by the parents' opposing accounts, found herself scrambling to ascertain out which parent was telling "the truth." She fantasized about hiring a private detective to determine which parent had an affair. Trapped in bewilderment, therapists can slide into a defensive stance of omnipotence, concluding that the confusion reflects *their* lack of insight or effort, instead of recognizing they are caught in a bind created by the parents. By blaming themselves for their confusion, they defensively keep at bay a troubling confrontation with the parents' severe psychological disturbance. Because of acute discomfort and a natural inclination to establish clarity, therapists may leap into an alliance with one parent and then rationalize their choice (by convincing themselves that the other parent is more psychologically disturbed, for example). They may be out of touch with their underlying drive to resolve unbearable tensions.

Figuring out what is going on in a high-conflict divorce situation is challenging even when a therapist has access to the whole family. When a therapist does not, it requires even more patience and a greater willingness to tolerate ambiguity until the situation becomes clearer.

> *Ms. Udall, two years after a nasty divorce, sought help dealing with what she vaguely described as her ex-husband's persistent antagonism. Her therapist, experienced with high-conflict divorces, was wary. He wanted to help Ms. Udall but did not want to exacerbate a contentious family situation by simply agreeing with her in what he thought might be her defensive need to exaggerate her ex-husband's liabilities.*
>
> *In Ms. Udall's weekly sessions, the therapist listened carefully to her descriptions of her ex-husband's behaviors. Ms. Udall brought in emails her ex-husband had sent her, referring to her as a "bitch" and a "whore." While Ms. Udall was upset at the emails, she wondered if she were exaggerating her ex-husband's disturbance. She related, almost in passing, that her ex-husband had followed her a few times when she went on dates. She found this behavior troubling but, again, worried she might be "overreacting."*

It became clear to the therapist that Ms. Udall's primary problem was not a defensive need to exaggerate her ex-husband's psychopathology, as many high-conflict parents do, but the opposite: She defensively downplayed the depth of her ex-husband's disturbance because she found it so unsettling and scary. If therapists choose to work with individual adults in the context of high-conflict divorces, they can use these patients' defenses as a guidepost to assess if they are warding off the painful feelings associated with loss by defensively *exaggerating* the ex-spouse's difficult qualities, or, alternatively, if they, like Ms. Udall, are defensively *downplaying* the ex-spouse's psychological problems because of difficulties bearing that harsh reality (see chapter 12).

Taking Time to Self-Reflect

In working with high-conflict families, it is important for clinicians to take the time to become aware as possible of the feelings and fantasies that arise in the course of their interactions with family members (Gunsberg, 2005). By slowing down to reflect, therapists can counteract potentially destructive impulses to respond to pressures. Ms. L., described above, found herself disliking Nathan's father, who was ebullient and self-absorbed, and considered that Nathan's mother must be offering the "accurate" version of events. Aware of the dynamics of high-conflict divorces, though, and open to self-reflection, she wondered if she were being pulled out of a neutral stance. Through consultation with a trusted colleague, Ms. L. realized she was responding to feeling inadequate because of her inability to clarify the true story. Recognizing that she would never be able to pin down the truth, Ms. L. decided to forge ahead anyway. She used her sense of perplexity to understand better what it was like for Nathan to try to manage his life while caught between his feuding parents (see chapter 11).

Seeking Consultation

By standing outside the immediate pushes and pulls that high-conflict parents exert, colleagues, like the one who assisted Ms. L., can help therapists keep their bearings when their emotional reactions threaten to undermine interventions. Because therapists working with rancorous divorces are vulnerable to putting themselves at risk for being sued or facing complaints against their licenses, it is also can be helpful to have an attorney available for consultation if ethical issues arise (for instance, a question about circumstances under which a therapist may communicate with a court).

Therapists also should consider seeking therapy for themselves if they find themselves struggling emotionally in their work with a high-conflict divorce.

Dr. S. was working closely with two highly antagonistic parents in an effort to help them reduce conflict and be more attentive to their school-age daughter whom he was seeing twice weekly in therapy. He found himself worn down by the parents' arguing and considered giving up on the parent meetings and working with the girl alone. In his own personal therapy, he was able to recognize that he actually felt enraged at the parents, especially the father, who tended to bully his ex-wife and, at times, Dr. S. as well. He realized that he feared he was going to explode in the sessions and say something outlandish to this man. He recognized that, in his fury, he had withdrawn from setting clearer limits on the father, thus himself contributing to the escalation of tensions in the sessions.

Taking a Systems Approach

Traumatic separations (involving violence, sudden departures) can consolidate into patterns of recrimination and retribution, so early intervention is essential (Johnston, Roseby, and Kuehnle, 2009). When a therapist sees conflict between parents escalate not just in degree but in kind (e.g., explosive exchanges, threats of violence), referral to the kind of professional who can intervene within an established structure and with the support of the court is in order. These authors argue that working without an overarching structure and purpose in high-conflict cases is a "prescription for disaster" (2009, p. 258). Accordingly, they recommend that all interventions take place within the structure of a court order that coordinates the activities of the professionals involved in the case and provide guidelines to that end.

For therapists who specialize in work with high-conflict divorce and are accustomed to collaborating within the structure of a court order, such an arrangement might feel natural and comfortable. For many others, though, especially those who primarily conduct individual therapy, that process runs contrary to their usual practice. It may not occur to them, caught up as they are in their individual work, that simply agreeing with their patients' perceptions of the marriage and divorce could exacerbate a deteriorating family situation. In stepping into a high-conflict divorce, however, they have clinical and ethical obligations to consider the impact of their interventions on the family as a whole.

Dr. S. received a telephone inquiry from a man who expressed interest in finding a therapist for his teenage son. The man indicated that he and his wife had recently gone through a very difficult divorce and his son was living equally with both parents. He complained that his ex-wife was harming his son through her "borderline" behaviors, and his son needed help. He hoped to meet the therapist first to see if she would be a good match.

When Dr. S. asked about the ex-wife's participation in the therapy, the man stated that his ex-wife probably would not be interested in participating because it would bring her mental disturbance out into the open. Dr. S. responded that she did not believe she could help unless the boy's mother was

involved, and said she would want to speak with her before she set up any
appointments. The man, irritated, told her to forget it and hung up.

During the phone call, Dr. S. became aware of a wish to help the adolescent boy, whom she pictured as being vulnerable and under siege. She considered briefly that she might meet with the father to see if she could persuade him to agree to a consultation with the entire family. However, uncomfortably aware that she might be drawn into a high-conflict family situation without the ability to intervene adequately, she decided not to engage under the father's terms.

HELPING TO COUNTERACT ESCALATION

Structuring Parents' Interactions

When both parents in a high-conflict divorce are willing and able to sit in a room together, therapists might choose to work with them together either as an adjunct to a child therapy or as a co-parenting intervention without the children. In either role, therapists can help them manage their co-parenting relationship by providing concrete suggestions for calming inflamed situations. One such suggestion might be that parents communicate by email because that limits the possibility of escalation and leaves a paper trail. I sometimes invite parents locked into inflammatory interactions to copy me on email communications so that I can give them feedback on how to minimize provocations. This process is a lot like editing an essay, helping parents pare communication down to the essential. If the parents talk by phone, they should do so in a room with the door closed, *after* the children have gone to bed. (I cannot say how many times I have heard children describe angry conversations they have overheard while their parents insist they were being discreet.)

If seeing each other tends to become inflammatory, parents should minimize or eliminate sightings altogether by arranging pick-ups or drop-offs at school or at the home of a willing relative or friend (where one parent can drop off the children and the other parent can pick them up fifteen minutes later). I often offer parents the analogy of volatile chemicals: When they get near each other, they explode. I recommend strongly to tense parents that they never try to raise issues spontaneously at transitions because their interactions quickly devolve into arguments. If the parents do maintain brief contact—at a sporting event, for instance—they should exchange civil greetings for the sake of decorum (and their children) and nothing more.

When parents are working together well, flexibility around the schedule (or other aspects of co-parenting) can be helpful to all family members. A parent might ask to swap appointed weekends with the children to accommodate a visit from an out-of-town guest. A few months later, the other parent might request a similar trade. High-conflict parents, however, can rarely manage flexibility because ambiguity leads to squabbling. In these cases it is often best to recommend that they follow their Judgment of Divorce to the letter. A therapist might use this unfortunate reality as an incentive to the parents to settle down and treat each other respectfully so that at some point they will be able to be more reciprocally flexible. A therapist also can point out that stable, predictable schedules will be best for their children, especially when tension levels are high.

Mobilizing Resources to Mitigate Feuding and Litigation

Therapists who do not feel comfortable working with high-conflict parents might refer them to one of many community-based programs—perhaps through the family court—that teaches parents skills in reducing conflict. Billings, Robbins, and Gordon (2008) describe one such program, "After the Storm," which rests on social learning and cognitive behavioral therapy. It seeks to help parents recognize components of ineffective versus effective problem solving so they can implement more mature, constructive methods of dealing with their ex-spouses; the program also seeks to help parents recognize thoughts that lead to anger so they can begin to change their habitual patterns of thinking. Pedro-Carroll, Nakhnikian, and Montes (2001) describe a program designed specifically to help parents at separation reduce the stress of their breakup on their children and learn skills to protect their children from the damaging effects of conflict. Neff and Cooper (2004) found that even a four-hour class for high-conflict parents can have a significant and enduring impact.

Parents in high-conflict divorces frequently seek redress in court in order to retaliate for perceived injustices at the hands of the spouse or to counteract feelings of shame by "winning" in a public forum. But litigation, in addition to being highly stressful, is extremely expensive, consuming precious financial resources that could be better applied elsewhere (e.g., therapy, children's education). Litigation takes problem-solving out of the hands of parents, which means they do not develop co-parenting skills. It usually exacerbates tensions because the adversarial system by its nature sharpens differences; parents often feel as if the process has slid out of control. In addition, judges usually lack the time, patience, and expertise to examine in detail the needs of individual children.

If therapists conceptualize immersion in litigation as a harmful avoidance of necessary mourning and disengagement, then, under most circumstances, they should work to help their patients avoid adversarial processes (Ehrlich, 2011). Therapists should be aware of the influence of the other professionals their patients are dealing with. For instance, if a parent hires a pugilistic attorney who is egging him or her on, the therapist might question whether such a choice is helpful. In recent years, the legal system, in response to a consensus that an adversarial system of law is ill-suited for family disputes and can damage children, has undergone a paradigm shift, moving toward a more collaborative, interdisciplinary approach (Singer, 2009). These evolving approaches to resolving conflicts offer new hope for divorcing spouses and provide therapists with useful options for referrals (and potential roles if they wish to expand their practices).

Notably, some family law attorneys now work toward a collaborative resolution of divorce-related conflicts over property and custody (Lande, 2011; Mosten, 2011). They often involve clinicians as "coaches" to help parents manage the stresses of the divorce process. By working collaboratively, the professionals counteract the adversarial tendencies that contribute to polarization and escalation, facilitating disengagement between the spouses. Collaborative practice uses a "disqualification provision" in which both lawyers are disqualified from representing their clients if the case ends up in litigation. The provision is designed to motivate all participants to stay engaged in what can often be a challenging process of negotiation.

Ms. D. was seeing Mr. Vale in individual therapy during his difficult divorce. While Mr. Vale was angry and hurt, he was also determined to get through the divorce with as little rancor and expense as possible in order to minimize stress for the children and to save money for education. Ms. D. suggested to him that, given those goals, a collaborative approach to the divorce might work best for him. Mr. Vale approached his wife with the idea and she agreed. Mr. Vale and his wife, despite fits and starts, were able to reach a divorce agreement over the following three months without involving the court.

When parental conflict is unremitting and damaging, a therapist might suggest the parent consider engaging a parenting coordinator—a clinician with expertise in high-conflict divorce who is court-appointed, has a non-confidential role vis-à-vis the court and the attorneys, and is mandated to help parents implement their parenting plan, monitor compliance, and assist with the timely resolution of child-related disputes. Parenting coordinators also can help parents problem-solve and negotiate more effectively, and can provide education regarding child-development issues (Deutsch, Coates, and Fieldstone, 2009). By having access to both parents and the opportunity to work with them over time, parenting coordinators typically can avoid aligning with one parent and contributing to escalation. Parenting coordinators work within the very specific guidelines of a court order that dictates what sorts of issues they will address. While they seek to negotiate resolution to conflicts, they also can make recommendations to the court if parents cannot reach agreement.

SOME DANGERS OF CHILD CUSTODY EVALUATIONS

In a small percentage of high-conflict divorces, families are ordered by the court to undergo custody evaluations in order to resolve custody disputes. Custody evaluations may be useful in finally resolving such disputes when they have dragged on. Unfortunately, though, such evaluations rarely help feuding parents get along better and often contribute to polarization. Although custody evaluators have access to all family members and, presumably, understand the dynamics of the high-conflict divorce, they too can have trouble navigating the bewildering experience of dealing with troubled parents who offer diverging versions of the same circumstances. Some child custody reports conclude, essentially, that one parent is good and one parent is bad, instead of offering a more nuanced assessment of complicated situations. Custody evaluators, despite their commitment to neutrality and emphasis on "objective" and "scientific" data, are subject, as all clinicians are, to the powerful pulls these parents exert, which can override other considerations. Negative reactions to one parent also can influence the outcome of these evaluations (Gunsberg, 2005).

> *Mr. Wills, at the time of the divorce five years ago, got into a violent confrontation with his teenage son and then, deeply distraught, fled the state for two weeks. Meanwhile, Ms. Wills found a therapist to diagnose Mr. Wills as psychotic and dangerous, so when Mr. Wills returned to the state he was only able to see the children with supervision and could not convince anyone he did not present a danger. Two custody evaluators found Ms. Wills' views of the family situation to be accurate: She was a devoted mother earnestly seeking to protect her children from a disturbed man.*
>
> *When Mr. Wills was able to successfully obtain a third evaluation, the evaluator was astonished to see how polarized the views of the first two evaluators and also therapists and court personnel had become. She found that Mr. Wills was somewhat labile and had a gruff, curt manner that others, understandably, saw as unpleasant and confusing, but she also found that Ms. Wills, whose portrayal of herself as essentially faultless had persuaded the other evaluators to favor her, was an extremely angry, vindictive woman invested in representing her ex-husband in the harshest terms possible. The third evaluator's more balanced assessment was met with disdain by Ms. Wills and her attorney, as well as court personnel.*

The third evaluator's assessment of the family situation spoke more than the previous custody reports did to the emotional issues underlying the tragedy of a father's having been pushed out of his children's lives and of two parents' incapacity to find a constructive path through divorce. The other professionals found it much more comfortable, perhaps even gratifying, to jump on the bandwagon of the mother's reductionistic narrative of protecting her children from a "crazy" man.

Mental health professionals' alignment with a parent's retaliatory fury functions psychologically for them as it does for parents: It distances them from awareness of the terrible losses in high-conflict families as well as feelings of helplessness in the face of intractable conflict. In a case such as Mr. and Ms. Wills, it also is easy for professionals to be swayed by one parent's more overt symptoms. Mr. Wills' unpleasantness, as well as his volatile behaviors around the separation, made it easier for professionals to assume he was *the* disturbed parent. In contrast, Ms. Wills' dispassionate, articulate account of her ex-husband's disturbance, which masked the depth of her psychological disturbance, made it easier for professionals to sympathize with her.

Divorcing people often make attribution errors in response to a spouse's troubled behaviors at separations, assuming they reflect fundamental character flaws in the spouse, as opposed to situational reactions to stress. Such people are prone to reify their observations and consolidate a vision of the other spouse as more disturbed than she or he actually is (Johnston and Campbell, 1988). Mental health professionals often make the same attribution errors. In this particular case, they seized on Mr. Wills' troubled behaviors during the highly stressful weeks around the separation and concluded he was violent and out of control (which he was not).

"PARENTAL ALIENATION SYNDROME"

One of the most disturbing, inflammatory phenomena that therapists come across in working with high-conflict divorces involves what has been called "parental alienation syndrome." As the phenomenon was originally described in the literature (Gardner, 1998), one parent in a divorce situation, through egregious, unremitting manipulation of a child (or through disturbed enmeshment), leads the child to turn hatefully against the other parent and cease contact. Some situations in which children resist contact with a parent are, in fact, straightforward: avoidance of an abusive parent, for example, or the result of deliberate alienation. Recent discussions on the topic, however, suggest that a child's estrangement from a parent in high-conflict divorce rarely involves simple manipulation by the other parent (Fidler and Bala, 2010). Most involve multiple, intersecting factors (Kelly and Johnston, 2001), whose complexity professionals often reduce to the simplistic. Such reductionisim on the part of professionals mirrors the tendency of high-conflict parents to reduce complex family matters to "good" vs. "bad" (Fidler and Bala, 2010).

In my clinical experience, the phenomenon of a child refusing contact with a parent is, indeed, usually extremely complicated and rarely fits into a clear framework of one parent victimizing the other. Instead, both parents play a role by entrapping the child in an impossible bind by engaging in highly polarizing, unremitting conflict in which each asserts that the other is the bad parent who is responsible for the family turmoil. Children, buffeted by parental conflict for years, are unable to create a safe middle space between their parents. Eventually, overwhelmed, they leap to an alliance with one parent. That parent then feels vindicated that she or he was right about the other parent's impossible qualities and denies a role in the child's suffering. The parent pushed to the periphery asserts furiously that the other parent turned the child against him or her and denies a role in the child's suffering.

In the cases I have seen, in keeping with other clinicians' reports, once children jump into one parent's camp, their antagonism toward the other parent is ferocious and unrelenting: In their minds, the rejected parent is "bad" and "unworthy," and they adamantly refuse to reconsider such conclusions, even in the face of contrary evidence.

> *Chuck, twelve, went back and forth between his parents' home for two years after his parents' bitter divorce that followed a tumultuous marriage. Mr. Yates and Ms. Yates continually litigated issues of property and the parenting arrangement. He, a loud man with a bad temper, referred to her as a "controlling bitch" in Chuck's presence. She countered furiously (also in Chuck's presence) that he was "carousing with whores" and warned Chuck not to catch any diseases from the bathroom. One evening, Chuck quietly left his father's house and walked four miles to his mother's house. He later told a therapist that his mother was right; he had determined that his father was "a complete jerk," and said he was done with that relationship.*

In the months that followed, a therapist tried to intervene to no avail. Chuck insisted that his father was a "corrupt son of a bitch" who had never loved him and that he was never going to see him again. Mr. Yates, contending that he was the victim of "parental alienation syndrome," accused Chuck's mother of viciously brainwashing Chuck to hate him, and was unable to acknowledge that his angry tirades had affected his relationship with his son. Ms. Yates countered that she actually supported Chuck's relationship with Mr. Yates but that Chuck had found out for himself what a terrible man his father was. She could not acknowledge that her outbursts about Mr. Yates's "whores" influenced Chuck's view of his father. The parents' attorneys filed motions and counter-motions, arguing for and against the view that Chuck was the victim of his mother's machinations.

Mr. Yates loved Chuck and was heartbroken by his refusal to see him. He had exploded angrily at Chuck a few times and had spoken badly about Ms. Yates, but he had never become violent. He had logged many hours with his son and coached several of his sports teams. Chuck's total dismissal of his father's commitment represented a gross distortion of reality, typical of children in these situations who deny ever having experienced good times with the rejected parent (Fidler and Bala, 2010). Ms. Yates was delighted that Chuck was living with her, which she saw as vindication of her views of Mr. Yates. Although she stated publicly that Chuck needed to work out a relationship with his father, what she said to Chuck in private could not be known.

The consulting psychologist found that Chuck felt torn apart by his parents' feud. He had come to feel, literally, as if he were losing his mind. After years of torment, unable to tolerate feeling caught between warring parents, Chuck leapt to his mother's side, aligning himself with her view of Mr. Yates (which dovetailed in part with his own) and defensively disavowing any loving feelings for his father.

In some instances, children reunite spontaneously with an estranged parent when life circumstances change—for example, a graduation or illness of a family member (Johnston and Goldman, 2010). Not surprisingly, given the inflammatory nature of these situations, efforts at intervention are complicated and sometimes controversial. For instance, professionals disagree over the extent to which court involvement in interventions is helpful and necessary (Fidler and Bala, 2010) Experts on children estranged from a parent often recommend comprehensive and multi-faceted interventions (as opposed, for instance, to individual child therapy), consistent with the multiple intersecting layers of these situations. Accordingly, clinicians have designed intensive programs to help estranged children reestablish relationships with their parents (Warshak, 2010; Sullivan, Ward, and Deutsch, 2010).

Chapter Eleven

Individual Therapy with Children and Adolescents Dealing with Divorce

SOME FUNCTIONS OF CHILD THERAPY
IN DIVORCE SITUATIONS

While working with parents is critical to helping children of divorce, therapists can also help children through individual therapy, especially when parents are having a hard time helping the child themselves. Therapists can help children communicate more effectively with their parents regarding whatever aspects of the divorce are stressing them; doing so is often a problem-solving task that may have interpretive elements as well (for instance, helping with unconscious inhibitions against speaking freely). Therapists also can apply information gleaned from individual child sessions to inform their work with parents. The better they understand the child, the more refined their parent guidance will be. Finally, therapists can help a child come to terms with his or her internal conflicts regarding the divorce. More specifically, child therapy can facilitate children's mourning by helping them confront and come to terms with painful realities they have defensively avoided.

A Multi-Layered Intervention: Therapy with Dan, Age Ten

Dan's parents sought help for Dan, ten, because he was increasingly angry and argumentative at home. Though they had divorced four years earlier, the parents still bickered about aspects of Dan's care, including who was responsible for paying for his activities. Each told Dan that the other parent was being cheap. Dan became morose and moody and began arguing with his parents about their "stupid rules." In turn, they took away his computer privileges and told him to get his act together.

The therapist initially met a few times with Dan's parents, who began squabbling as soon as they entered his office. Though both were invested in Dan's well-being, they conceded they had a tense relationship that seeped into interactions with Dan. They agreed to work with the therapist to try to diminish their arguing and agreed the therapist would see Dan in weekly sessions.

Over the course of those individual sessions, the therapist, after learning more about Dan's experience of his parents' households, worked gently with Dan's defenses, suggesting to him that it is easier for boys to argue with their parents than it is to slow down and think about how disappointing and frustrating it feels when parents are at odds. The therapist strove to put into words what Dan's parents were unable to say to him because they were too absorbed in struggling with each other: They, still caught up in their feelings about the divorce, were behaving in ways that would be upsetting and disappointing for any child. Dan, relieved that the therapist had found words for his experience, began to talk about his amazement that even four years after their divorce his parents were still arguing, and he wondered aloud: "Why aren't they over it yet?" The therapist explained to Dan that some parents have a really hard time getting over the end of a marriage and, in an effort to help Dan feel freer to acknowledge his sorrow, the therapist talked about how sad that was for his whole family.

Dan then began to speak about his sense of failure at his inability to get his parents to settle down. For years, he had hoped that, if he did not ask for too much (for example, new soccer cleats), his parents would have less to tangle about. Finally, when he realized his approach had no impact, he gave up trying and turned to confrontation. The therapist spoke with Dan about how disappointing it was not to be able to affect his parents more. He suggested that this unfortunate circumstance did not reflect Dan's failure but, instead, derived from his parents' inability to get over the divorce. He spoke about how urgently Dan, a thoughtful boy, wanted to see his parents calm down and feel better and how hard it was for him to bear the helplessness that comes with realizing how limited his influence is. This last intervention addressed Dan's omnipotent defense against his helplessness: his fantasy that he could influence his parents and his concomitant conviction that he failed because his parents still argued.

In order to help Dan comprehend the family situation and counteract his sense that the parents' failure was his, not theirs, the therapist was determined to speak directly to the upsetting fact that Dan's parents *had* failed to manage their co-parenting relationship effectively. At the same time, he wanted to frame the parents' predicament in ways that helped Dan understand and empathize with it—working carefully, in other words, not to ally with Dan against his parents by maligning them.

Alongside his individual therapy with Dan, the therapist worked with Dan's parents to help them better understand Dan's experience. He explained that Dan, understandably, was angry because he felt disappointed and helpless in the face of their arguing. They needed to set limits on Dan when he escalated in his behaviors, but they also needed to work to change the stressful home life they were subjecting him to. The therapist used the information he gained from the individual therapy with Dan to inform his consultation with Dan's parents; first, however, he discussed this approach with Dan who agreed it would be useful for his parents to understand what was going on in the therapy. They agreed on what the therapist could discuss with the parents so Dan could maintain some domains of privacy. Simultaneously, the therapist helped Dan find ways that he himself could let his parents know how troubling he found it when they argued. Because he was anxious about speaking to them, Dan needed encouragement and support and even specific suggestions for what he might say.

Bearing Painful Affects when Parents Cannot: Therapy with Cynthia, Age Eight

> *Cynthia, eight years old, was reeling in response to her parents' separation. A quiet, reflective girl, she had known they had been tense and unhappy for the last year but had not anticipated they would split. She felt shattered that the family had come apart and worked obsessively to treat her parents equally in the hope that tensions would abate and they would reunite. Having cherished family time, especially summer weekends at the lake cottage, she was stunned when her parents talked about selling it. Though her parents knew Cynthia was upset, they seemed to avoid discussing with her what was going on.*

In the therapy with Cynthia, the therapist was aware of feeling that her sorrow was almost more than he could bear. He found Cynthia to be an exceptionally caring, gentle girl who was highly invested in having a happy family. He was moved by her absorption in being fair to her parents, which reflected both her tenderness and her desperate wish to alter the course of fate. The therapist found himself wanting to parent Cynthia, to step into the void created by her parents' divorce and provide this suffering girl with solace. Nonetheless, he worked with Cynthia's omnipotent fantasy that her careful, thoughtful behaviors would influence her parents' decision so that she could begin to deal with her powerlessness to intervene, perhaps the most excruciating aspect of her experience. He asked Cynthia what she had loved about family time and worked to bear her sorrow about its coming to an end. Simultaneously, he worked with Cynthia to consider establishing new traditions in her newly reconstituted family, including new rituals for summer weekends.

That intervention with Cynthia is consistent with Tessman's (1996) observation that mastery of depression has two components: tolerating the experience of helplessness at being unable to alter certain painful realities and mobilizing resources to reinvest in new sources of gratification that are, indeed, possible. In working with children of divorce, then, therapists need to balance children's need to bear sorrow with some glimmers of light at the end of the tunnel. Helping children develop new tools—such as speaking up assertively in response to divorce-related stressors—helps to counteract their feelings of helplessness.

Other Functions of Child Therapy in Divorce

Tessman (1996) notes that children use identification with the absent (or mainly absent) parent as a means of coping with loss. Such identifications can lead to emotional and behavioral difficulties and can impede investment in new relationships. Thus therapy with children and adolescents who have lost (or essentially lost) parents often involves exploring and then working through defensive identifications with the missing parent so a constructive mourning process can begin. Chethik et al. (1987) cite the role of identifications with negative aspects of the missing parent after divorce. Such "negative identifications" (p. 121) serve various defensive functions for children: fending off the sadness in object loss, managing the anxiety of helplessness, dealing with abandonment, warding off threatening aspects of the self, and protecting against diminished self-esteem.

> *Jerome, twelve, saw his father for occasional weekends and for a few weeks each summer after his parents divorced when he was seven years old. He longed for more contact but his father, remarried, focused most of his energy on his new wife and their infant. Jerome's father tended to be macho in his mode of interacting, which included a patronizing stance toward women. When Jerome returned from visits with his father, he often sounded macho himself and spoke down to his mother.*

In this particular situation, Jerome's identification with his father protected him from his anguish that his father had turned his attention to a new child. Therapists can work directly with children to understand these negative identifications and also help the remaining parent understand and address them productively.

Chethik and Kalter (1980) assert that divorce can interrupt basic developmental tasks, leaving children searching for primary attachments. In their view, the therapist in post-divorce therapy serves as a "real object" for the child more than is typical in child therapy. They describe the therapist as a "developmental facilitator" (p. 286), that is, one who allows the child to experience and negotiate developmental tasks that were disrupted by the loss of or diminished contact with a parent. Lohr et al. (1981) suggest that giving up the parental unit is a painful task for children coping with divorce, and that children need help in therapy dealing with persistent fantasies of reconciliation in order to mourn the loss of that parental unit. The outcome of all of these interventions can be enriched by an engaged, empathic parent.

INDIVIDUAL THERAPY WITH ADOLESCENTS

While many adolescents complain about grown-ups trying to intrude in their lives and act as if they do not need help, they are often very amenable to engaging in individual therapy and, if they feel understood, are quick to open up.

Caught in the Immediate Aftermath of Divorce: Therapy with Carol, Age Eighteen

> *After a strained marriage, Carol's parents, suddenly in her eyes, told her that they were getting a divorce. In short order, the parents sold the family home in which Carol had grown up, and her mother bought a new one. Carol, in her first year of college, asked to see a therapist. Carol told the therapist in the first session that she was confused about why she was so upset by the news of her parents' divorce and the sudden changes in her parents' lives. After all, she said, she was eighteen years old and had moved out of the house and begun a new life.*

The therapist responded that he did not think it was so surprising. Yes, she was eighteen years old and appeared to be a capable young woman adjusting to that new life, but eighteen-year-olds still need their parents and rely on familiar routines. When the therapist mentioned familiar routines, Carol, essentially given permission to acknowledge her dependence on her parents, became tearful and said she was not sure what was going to happen for the holidays. Thanksgiving was coming up and, despite her parents' tensions, that had been a special time in the family. Her parents were so caught up in the divorce that no one had mentioned Thanksgiving, much less Christmas. She had thought about asking her parents about family plans but was reluctant to burden them.

Over the next few months, Carol was able to acknowledge that her parents' tensions had troubled her for a long time. She also expressed concern that she had been damaged by a model for intimate relationships that failed. The therapist reassured her that nothing was written in stone about her relationships and that she could get help with her future relationships if she found herself having difficulty. Much of the focus was on Carol's hesitancy to engage her parents to come up with plans around college events (such as Parents' Weekend) and holidays that would work for Carol. When Carol expressed guilt that by pressing her parents she was adding to their already significant strain, the therapist pointed out that, the divorce notwithstanding, they were still responsible as parents to come up with arrangements that, at least in part, addressed Carol's needs. This topic then lead to an important exploration of Carol's tendency to take too much responsibility for others' feelings and, in doing so, lose track of her own.

Guilt Around Leaving: Therapy with Cory, Age Seventeen

In chapter 6, we got a brief glimpse of Cory, whose parents' inability to manage their lives post-divorce left him crippled with guilt, which he tried to manage through daily marijuana use and video games. Cory was typical of teenagers in that he was initially unaware of how much his family life, including his parents' divorce, had affected him; rather, he presented a vague sense of unhappiness and a feeling that he could not move ahead with his life, focusing on school and his intense dislike of homework.

After a few sessions, when the therapist noted he rarely said anything about his family, Cory spoke of the divorce for the first time and began weeping so hard he could not talk for several minutes. Cory was taken aback by the intensity of his sorrow, which, he and the therapist came to understand, he had effectively blocked out by denying its existence and smoking marijuana. Cory noted that he had never spoken to anybody about the divorce, other than to mention it in passing.

Over the next several months, as Cory and the therapist worked to understand what about the divorce felt so painful, Cory was able to articulate that his parents had been unable to recover from the devastation of their breakup. He wept in recalling happy family times when he was a little boy. The therapy then focused on Cory's overweening sense of responsibility for his parents, which led him to feel he was not entitled to have a thriving life of his own. Cory and the therapist came to recognize that Cory had effected a defensive identification with his parents' dysfunction: He unconsciously took on as his own their inadequacy in coping with their lives as a way to block out his sorrow about their chronic depression and disappointing qualities. As Cory was able to begin to mourn how devastating the divorce had been to his parents and how much he, too, had lost, he began to feel freer to create a lively, successful life that was different from theirs.

INTEGRATING PARENTS INTO ADOLESCENTS' THERAPY

The brilliant television series *Friday Night Lights* captures beautifully the roles that adults play in the lives of adolescents. The teenagers in a rural Texas town engage in passionate, complex relationships with their parents as they struggle to find their own identities. High school students repeatedly show up at the house of the football coach and his wife—sometimes in the middle of the night—seeking nurturance and wisdom from a couple that functions as a stand-in for absent or unavailable parents.

When parents are, indeed, absent or unavailable, therapists, as well as other adults like the coach and his wife, can function as substitute parents. Hetherington and Kelly (2002) found that one shared feature of all of the successful children in their study of divorce was the support of at least one caring and loving adult. They suggest that mentors can play such a role by modeling appropriate behaviors and offering advice. For a therapist, providing a parental function that is lacking is a powerful and important role. In that connection I recall working with a young adolescent who had been left to his own devices after his mother died and his father withdrew into a protracted grieving. As part of the therapy, I explained to him how to bake chicken. But when parents are available to participate in their adolescent's therapy, it is critical to help work out the best relationship possible between them because parents spend each day interacting with their children, whereas therapists see them for brief periods each week. Besides, committed parents will be involved in their children's lives long after therapy ends.

Enhancing Communication Between Teenager and Parent

Divorcing parents often worry tremendously about growing rifts with their adolescent children. Helping them repair a strained or distant relationship can be a powerful intervention. It can be effected through individual sessions with the adolescent and collateral sessions with parents or sessions with adolescents and parents together.

> *Gail, thirteen, spoke often in her individual therapy about her hurt feelings and anger toward her father who seemed content to play a secondary role in her life. During their alternating-weekend visits, she was often withdrawn or dismissive toward him. She was, however, open to having father/daughter sessions. During the joint sessions, Gail's father, with the therapist's encouragement, told Gail that he felt hurt because he experienced her distancing from him as a lack of investment in their relationship. Gail then explained that she withdrew at her father's house because she believed that he was not especially interested in spending time with her.*

Here, the therapist was able to address a common problem between parent and teenager in divorce situations—a basic lack of communication—by helping father and daughter speak openly to each other. Both Gail and her father learned vital information about the other that opened the door to them having a closer relationship.

Countertransference Traps in Working with Adolescents

When therapists fail to include parents in interventions, they run a serious risk of exacerbating difficult situations by enlarging the space between parent and child.

> *Ms. Zane sought therapy for her son, Bill, fourteen, after a difficult divorce. She worried about his rage, especially his tendency to verbally abuse her. Bill angrily complained to the therapist about his parents' inadequacy for failing to work out their marriage and their continued tensions. The therapist was taken in by Bill's vivid account of his parents' insensitivity. Empathizing with Bill's distress, he aligned himself with Bill's sense of victimization.*
>
> *Meanwhile, Bill's behaviors were escalating at home. His verbal abuse of his mother increased and he began to bully children at school. The therapist, who believed he had a good grasp on the family situation, chose not to meet with the parents and thus failed to address the growing problems at home. Ms. Zane, feeling increasingly besieged and misunderstood and, finally, enraged at the lack of help with Bill's behaviors, pulled Bill from therapy. The therapist, out of touch with Ms. Zane as he was, felt hurt and angry when she suddenly terminated the therapy.*

The trouble in situation like this one often derives from therapists' countertransference difficulties: Identified with their child and adolescent patients, therapists play out unconscious scripts in which they vicariously express their anger and hurt toward their *own parents*. Bill's therapist, reflecting later on the breakdown of the therapy, recognized with some anguish that he had taken pleasure in Bill's expression of hostility toward his parents. He conceded that had he taken the time to get to know Bill's parents, he might have learned they were not nearly as inadequate as Bill presented them to be and, perhaps, could have received a well-reasoned explanation for why they dealt with their son as they did in response to his difficult behaviors. Adolescents often project their own sense of badness onto their parents, distorting the reality of their parents' intent. When therapists simply assume that adolescents' portrayal of their parents is accurate, they may reinforce the adolescent's acting-out behaviors, as in the case of Bill.

Therapists, because of their sensitivity toward the feelings of their adolescent patients, can become judgmental toward parents and lose track of challenges parents face in trying to manage difficult teenagers. Therapists working with children and adolescents need to carefully examine their own motivations for their work, including looking at their inevitably unresolved feelings about their own parents. Sometimes awful family situations are unambiguous: Insensitive parents are mistreating or even abusing children or adolescents. But frequently, bad situations are the product of more than one dynamic, as the difficult behaviors of children and adolescents—verbally or physically abusing parents—contribute to and compound family problems (Price, 1996).

Helping to Coordinate Care Between an Adolescent's Parents

Coordination of care becomes especially critical with adolescents. A therapist can help parents understand that while many adolescents protest rules and regulations and try to drive a wedge between tense parents, most need structure and feel reassured when parents come together to contain them. Unless divorced parents are being draconian in their strictures, it often is best to tilt in the direction of too much containment for a teenager as opposed to too little because most adolescents, protestations aside, experience containment as a reflection of their parents' love and concern, especially when parents have been pulled apart by a divorce.

> *Celine was outraged when her mother insisted that she could not be alone with her boyfriend at his house when his parents were away. After all, she was now fifteen years old and her father did not monitor her as closely when she stayed with him. When Celine's mother confronted her father about his leniency, he criticized her for being too uptight because he believed Celine was old enough to make such decisions for herself.*

It became clear to Celine's therapist that she felt overwhelmed by the possibility of having sex with her boyfriend and did not feel ready to negotiate the issue on her own, even though she argued the opposite. In working with Celine's parents, the therapist concentrated on her developmental need for clear, firm, and consistent guidelines from *both parents* about appropriate behaviors and issues of safety. The therapist tried to avoid the appearance of being allied with Celine's mother, even though he agreed with her, by focusing on Celine's more general need for constraints. When Celine's father altered his stance and agreed with his ex-wife about rules for the boyfriend's house, Celine reacted with disgust and outrage. It was evident to the therapist, though, that she was privately relieved that her parents had come together as a united front and were keeping her from running amok.

Therapists should be willing to tell parents that their current parenting arrangement is not working, especially when a breakdown in communication puts the adolescent at risk.

> *A year before seeking a consultation with a therapist, Mr. Ash and Ms. Ash committed to a 50/50 parenting arrangement for their two teenage daughters. However, after about six months, Melissa, thirteen, a bright girl, began failing out of school. The parents, alarmed, blamed each other. Mr. Ash was convinced that Melissa had ADHD and needed medication; Ms. Ash was adamantly opposed. Neither would budge. When her parents brought her in to*

meet the therapist, Melissa, desperate, complained that she needed help but her parents could not agree on anything.

The therapist, after meeting twice with the parents and seeing how entrenched their conflict was, told them she did not think she could help Melissa until they found a way to coordinate care. She suggested that they consider one of two options: work with a mediator to help them arrive at a decision for Melissa or alter their parenting arrangement so that one parent had primary responsibility. The parents opted for mediation and agreed to return later for Melissa's therapy.

INDIVIDUAL THERAPY WITH LATE ADOLESCENTS/YOUNG ADULTS

Therapists working with young adults around divorce, often (and appropriately) keep parents on the periphery in order to forge an alliance with a young person who is intent on maintaining as much autonomy as possible. In divorcing families with considerable tensions, however, including parents can be helpful toward mobilizing their support for the therapy, creating a forum for addressing parenting issues, and gaining information for diagnostic reasons.

Tammy, a twenty-two-year-old college senior, expressed frustration in therapy that her parents, in the midst of a divorce, were "off the wall." Even though they were wealthy professionals, she said, they constantly complained about paying for her therapy, despite her obvious suffering. Tammy felt abandoned and bereft. The therapist felt perplexed and wondered if Tammy's high-powered parents could be as dysfunctional as she indicated.

When the issue of payment for therapy came to a head, the therapist invited Tammy's mother to meet with him and Tammy together to see if they could come up with a plan. Tammy's mother forlornly stated that her husband had destroyed her financially. She told Tammy and the therapist not to expect much from her because she could barely manage her own life.

In this context it was extremely helpful for the therapist to meet the parent and get a clearer sense of what the young person was dealing with. While some late adolescents and young adults exaggerate their parents' difficulties, Tammy's bleak report about her mother was accurate. Fortified with that background information, the therapist could help Tammy grieve her mother's dysfunction and its impact on her parenting.

INDIVIDUAL THERAPY IN THE HIGH-CONFLICT DIVORCE WITH CHILDREN AND ADOLESCENTS

Managing Confusion: Therapy with Nathan, Age Eleven

In chapter 10, we met Nathan, eleven, a boy whose divorced parents argued about which parent was having an affair. Nathan's therapist, Ms. L., herself struggled to come to terms with her inability to resolve the ambiguity. Once she identified her own bewilderment, Ms. L. decided to tell Nathan that she herself could not figure out what was going on with the parents, despite her efforts. Nathan had felt "stupid" for being unable to figure out which parent's story was accurate and was enormously relieved to learn that this intelligent social worker was as confused as he was.

Through therapy, Nathan began to see that the problem did not derive from *his* inadequacy but from his parents' incapacity to provide a consistent narrative. Ms. L. was able to help Nathan begin to deal with his feelings about that disturbing fact. She also was able to give him a framework for understanding what was going on by explaining how parents in difficult divorces often get caught up in their own views and have a hard time considering another person's. Finally, she and Nathan devised strategies for his talking to the parents about not wanting to hear about their personal lives.

Ms. L.'s therapy with Nathan illustrates an essential feature of individual therapy with children in high-conflict divorces. When parents are caught up in protracted conflict, children need support and, further, some guided reality testing toward making sense of the family situation. Nathan's omnipotent fantasy (i.e., his conviction that it was because of his inadequacy that he could not make sense of the situation) diminished his sense of competence and undermined his adaptation. As he began to let go of his defensive blaming of himself and see that the problem lay with his parents, Nathan felt more competent, though he had to begin to consider just how troubled his parents were.

Johnston and Campbell (1988), in describing short-term interventions with children entrapped in high-conflict divorces, emphasize the need to help them attain some psychological distance from their parents' dispute, find ways to maintain positive relationships with both parents, and resume their own development. They also emphasize the importance of explaining in simple, concrete language what is going on with the court and custody and providing explanations in a non-blaming way so as not to alienate these children from their parents. In addition, the authors describe helping these children develop coping skills, based on the assumption that the parents' feuding will be protracted.

Struggling to Carve out a Middle Space: Therapy with Cassie, Age Nine

Cassie, nine, was brought to therapy by her parents who were engaged in a longstanding dispute over custody. Her mother, furious at her father for initiating the divorce, frequently criticized Cassie's father in front of Cassie, referring to him as "controlling" and a "miserable dad" and blaming him aloud for their breakup. Cassie's father defended himself, telling Cassie that her mother was "mean" and insisting that she, not he, was responsible for the divorce.

The therapist engaged Cassie in a brief therapy and, in addition, referred the parents to a parenting coordinator to curb their feuding and develop more empathy for their daughter. Cassie, in her individual sessions, spoke about her parents' "angry words" and her anxious feeling that much of the time she could not make sense of the divorce because her mother and father told her different things. The therapist empathized with Cassie, remarking that girls end up feeling very confused when their parents tell them different things. Cassie agreed, then described an alliance with her mother, noting that she and her mother "think dad is trying to control mom." She remarked that her father made up "pretty, pretty bad lies." She then said she did not know whether her dad or mom was "right," but she had decided to "go with my mom." The therapist offered that when girls are so confused, it feels awful, so they want to choose one parent because it makes things feel less confusing. Cassie nodded and then went on to say how hard it was to be her, and how other kids at school "don't have parents that lie about each other." Over the next five sessions, the therapist explained to Cassie how parents who are mad at each other often accuse each other of things. He told Cassie she did not have to agree with one parent or the other but could make up her own mind over time as to what was going on. He also worked with Cassie to find language to tell her parents to stop when one started speaking negatively about the other.

Struggling to Come to Terms with a Parent's Psychological Problems: Therapy with Grant, Age Fifteen

Therapists working with children and adolescents in high-conflict divorce situations function to clarify reality in language that children can absorb and no one is helping them sort out. This process includes working with the child's defenses against recognizing and integrating difficult features of the situation. In order to assist children in this task, therapists themselves must achieve clarity, which often means spending enough time with the parents that the therapist understands what is going on.

Grant, fifteen, lived primarily with his father after his parents divorced when he was twelve years old. Following some weekly visits with his mother, Grant gradually cut out even that contact and refused to go on visits altogether. Grant's father described Grant's mother as "crazy" and said he was unwilling to pressure his son to see her. The mother meanwhile told the therapist that Grant's father was turning Grant against her because he was still angry that she initiated the divorce.

Initially, the therapist found that, Grant, though bright, could only offer a vague account of why he did not want to see his mother. He said she sometimes was "mean" and said "nasty things" about his father. While Grant found such behaviors upsetting, he felt guilty that he was not spending more time with her and torn that he was hurting her, especially when she complained on the phone that Grant was breaking her heart. Grant struggled with an anguished feeling that he could work things out with her mother if he tried harder. He appreciated his father's support but did not quite trust his perceptions because he was, as his mother insisted, still angry about the breakup.

The therapist, confused, met with Grant's father, who told him that he wanted to support Grant's relationship with his mother but found it hard to do so because his ex-wife was vindictive and verbally abusive. The therapist, accustomed to such narratives in tense divorces, arranged meetings between Grant and his mother. His intent was twofold: to help them improve their relationship and to see if he could gain some clarity about their rift. In the joint sessions, the therapist was jolted by the harshness of Grant's mother. She accused Grant of not loving her and destroying her life. She told Grant that she was going to move out of state and he would never see her again. When Grant wept, his mother ignored him. When the therapist pointed out how her words were wounding Grant, she responded that he did not begin to understand the situation and should focus instead on the machinations of Grant's father, who was involved in a "conspiracy" to alienate her from her son.

While the therapist was invested in maintaining a positive relationship with both parents, he recognized that it was impossible in this particular situation. He worked in Grant's individual sessions to help him through the agonizing task of recognizing his mother's severe personality problems. He suggested to Grant that his sense of failure at not engaging his mother more successfully was a way to deny what he must know somewhere in his mind: His mother, for reasons that were unclear, had great difficulty being in relationships and treating people, including Grant, kindly. As Grant was able to find language to talk about his mother's difficulties more precisely, he became overwhelmed with sorrow that he had a mother who treated him so badly and could not provide the maternal functions he longed for.

While mourning these realities became the centerpiece of his therapy, the therapist also focused on helping Grant manage the relationship with his mother by setting strict limits when she became verbally abusive. Whereas Grant's tendency was simply to withdraw from his mother when she escalated, the therapist felt that withdrawal in the long run was not helpful because Grant would continue to feel that he had no control over the situation and would not develop adequate coping skills. Working together to determine which behaviors were unacceptable, they decided that verbal attacks on him or his father should not be tolerated. Grant would warn his mother once if she became verbally abusive and, if the abuse continued, he would end the conversation.

Grant occasionally backed away from the plan and allowed his mother to assault him verbally. At such times, the therapist focused on his guilt about setting limits on contact with her because even as Grant felt besieged by his mother's verbal assaults, he recognized that she was hurting terribly. That recognition put him in a bind that the therapist helped him articulate: He needed to create distance to protect himself but hurt his mother in doing so, and thus, in his mind, actualized his mother's accusation that he did not love her enough. Whenever guilt got the better of him, he succumbed to his mother's verbal assaults. Recognizing this dynamic allowed Grant to set limits more consistently.

Grant's sorrow about his mother's disturbance was wrenching for the therapist. He was aware of a wish to deny the mother's serious psychopathology, as Grant had done, because it rendered him, like Grant, helpless to intervene with the mother. He also was aware of a wish to tangle with Grant's mother, to confront her angrily about her mistreatment of Grant and lecture her on being a better mother. Reflecting on these impulses, he realized that the fantasy served to counteract his feelings of helplessness around intervening and his sorrow at Grant's predicament.

Still Struggling with a Puzzle: Therapy with Gabbie, Age Eighteen

Therapists also work with adolescents whose parents divorced many years earlier, but who find themselves still struggling to manage their related, ongoing distress.

> Gabbie, eighteen, dealing with her parents' divorce since she was three years old, seeks therapy as a first-year college student. She describes profound frustration that no matter how good she has become at solving complex math problems, she cannot solve a family mystery. Her mother still insists angrily that her father chose to leave the marriage because of another woman. Her father says this is one more instance of her mother's lies. Gabbie says, "I feel like I'm going crazy."

In therapy, Gabbie was able to explore her guilty, anxious feeling that she had allied herself more with her mother over the years because her mother owned a nicer house and offered her a car when she turned sixteen years old. The therapist was able to help her understand that the problem was not that she was selfish but that her parents had placed her in a bind by forcing her to choose one over the other. By expressing her confusion and finding the support of a neutral third party, Gabbie gradually became able to establish a more realistic view of her parents. She came to believe that her father, whom she found to be reliable and forthright, was probably offering a more accurate version of what happened at the separation, though she conceded he may have felt ashamed of his destructive behaviors and thus minimized or denied them. Gabbie felt that her mother, chronically embittered, was more likely to exaggerate. Gabbie was able to articulate her distress that she *never* would know what drove her parents apart, especially now that she was establishing an independent life outside her parents' home. She could also articulate her profound disappointment in her parents' inability to resolve their conflicts.

Chapter Twelve

Individual Therapy with Adults Dealing with Divorce

Some individuals seek out therapists when they are caught up in the momentous decision as to whether they should end their marriages. Others ask for help in the midst of a tumultuous ending to a marriage—the discovery of an affair, for instance. Still others ask for help when they find themselves struggling to come to terms with the end of their marriage, sometimes months or years after the marriage ended. Other than those situations in which prospective patients are coming in the middle of a crisis and therapy has the quality of crisis management, therapy with divorcing and recently divorced people usually revolves around mourning and barriers to mourning the end of the marriage. The process includes working with the person's defenses against painful underlying feelings and helping him or her to expand the capacity to tolerate those feelings.

FACILITATING MOURNING BY CONFRONTING DENIAL: MS. ADAMS

In chapters 1 and 2, we met Ms. Adams, for whom the disastrous collapse of her marriage recapitulated her early experience of dealing with a father with mental illness. Ms. Adams sought therapy when her relationship with her husband began to unravel. She was beginning to confront the fact that he was squandering their resources on cocaine and strip clubs but simultaneously wondered if she were exaggerating his liabilities. A bright, accomplished woman, Ms. Adams presented in a state of despair and bewilderment. She seemed unable to deploy her considerable intellectual resources to make sense of her predicament.

149

Ms. Adams, in the early stages of a four-times-per-week psychoanalysis, alternated between a focus on the positive features of her husband—his intelligence, business successes, self-confidence—and her sinking feeling that she had been taken in by him all along. She had found credit card receipts that indicated he was spending up to $1,000/month on strip clubs. She also saw evidence of cocaine use. At first, Ms. Adams had denied what she saw and assumed she must be exaggerating her concerns. As evidence accrued, though, she mustered the courage to confront her husband who told her that, yes, he want to strip clubs but it was for business purposes. He denied substance abuse and told Ms. Adams she was overreacting and needed to trust him. Shortly afterward, Ms. Adams received a shocking communication from her husband's business partner that suggested their business was floundering and was on the brink of bankruptcy.

The analyst found himself puzzled by Ms. Adams's confusion. While he had come to feel convinced that Ms. Adams's husband was escalating out of control and she was in danger of losing everything, the situation remained strangely unclear to her. She was unable to grasp it until, finally, a great deal of evidence accrued—whereupon she began to seesaw between bewilderment and a sense of catastrophic collapse when she realized that Mr. Adams was so different from the man she had imagined him to be.

Ms. Adams had been desperate to create a life with a stable, loving man and push the turmoil of her childhood as far in the past as possible. Seeing her father in a manic state had been so disturbing to Ms. Adams as a girl that she used to describe him to herself and others as "energetic" and "hyper," rather than as mentally ill. As her marriage began to crumble, she felt as if her life were falling apart once again. Her defensive need to deny her husband's problems tied in part to her childhood need to deny the devastating reality of her father's mental illness.

The analyst wondered during the early months of the treatment if Ms. Adams were exaggerating her husband's liabilities. Could Mr. Adams be so recklessly destructive? As time passed, however, and Ms. Adams brought in accumulating proof of her husband's problems, the analyst recognized that she was defensively shutting out awareness of his disturbed behaviors in a desperate effort to avoid facing the loss of the longed-for marital partner. The analyst realized he had colluded briefly with Ms. Adams: His inability to speak up and address the harsh reality before them paralleled her silence and, in addition, the behaviors of her mother, who, according to Ms. Adams, had never really acknowledged her father's mental illness with the result that Ms. Adams, while growing up, had no one to help her come to terms with it.

The analyst gradually began to confront Ms. Adams with her defensive denial. When she proposed that by making such a big deal she was being hysterical, he suggested that she would rather see herself as hysterical than acknowledge she was discerning something disturbing. Here, he was addressing Ms. Adams's omnipotent defenses: how she fantasized being responsible for her husband's disturbing behaviors in preference to feeling powerless. In other words, she was the problem, not he. When Ms. Adams denied the meaning of what she herself reported—for example, signs of cocaine use—the analyst observed that she preferred to relinquish the capacities of her excellent mind rather than allow herself to process the data in front of her. He compared her precision and acumen at work to her vagueness and uncertainty vis-à-vis her husband's behaviors.

Over the course of several months, Ms. Adams began to acknowledge more fully that her husband was out of control and her marriage was untenable and to confront her utter devastation at her betrayal by a man whom she needed. For months, the analyst and Ms. Adams worked through her profound feelings of sorrow and hurt. Her childhood loss of the father she had so wanted to be able to trust compounded her loss of the marital partner she had wanted to trust and complicated her mourning. Finally, she was able to see the facts before her clearly enough to separate from her husband and then, continuing to mourn, Ms. Adams filed for divorce.

FACILITATING MOURNING BY CONFRONTING DENIAL: MR. DOERR

While therapists see people like Ms. Adams who forestall mourning by denying the negative features of the spouse, they sometimes see people who are doing the opposite.

Mr. Doerr, a lawyer in his forties, immersed himself in a relationship with a woman at work whom he found exciting and enlivening. He was thrilled by their vigorous sex life and their trips to exotic locales. When he decided to divorce his wife, he felt relief at escaping a boring, exasperating marriage. He consulted a psychologist because, he said, he was worried about his teenage daughter who had begun acting out destructively.

In the initial consultation, Mr. Doerr contrasted the many pleasures of his new romance to his profound frustration with his wife, whom he described as harsh and critical. He gave no indication that he felt guilt that his affair had precipitated the end of his marriage, nor did he consider that his daughter's finding out about it was connected with the teenager's escalating acting-out behaviors. The psychologist sensed that Mr. Doerr was looking for help with more than his daughter, but also understood that she was a focus that would allow him to engage in therapy. They agreed to meet twice weekly.

In the first few weeks of the therapy, Mr. Doerr did focus on troubles with his daughter's behaviors but soon shifted attention to the stressful process of the divorce and his wife's difficult behaviors around the property settlement. Mr. Doerr indicated that the marital problems had gone on for a long time; he attributed them to his wife's inability to find meaningful work and feel good about herself. Their sex life had become non-existent in recent years, he said, as his wife withdrew from him into bitter isolation. Mr. Doerr expressed delight that his new lover was warm, kind, and uninhibited.

The therapist initially was taken in by Mr. Doerr's account of his wife, who came across as brittle, unpleasant, even retaliatory. He thought that Mr. Doerr was fortunate to have escaped such an unhappy marriage and found himself disliking Mr. Doerr's wife, whom he envisioned as a small, shrewish woman who would drive any man into the arms of another woman. Over time, though, as Mr. Doerr continued to paint a unidimensional picture of an unhappy marriage and a thrilling new relationship, the therapist sensed that the narrative was incomplete. Mr. Doerr often seemed subdued, even down, and his account seemed pat. The therapist realized he must be getting caught up in Mr. Doerr's defensive need to turn a complex situation, perhaps even a tragic one—a twenty-year marriage ending with his affair—into a purely positive one. He wondered, where is Mr. Doerr's sadness?

About a month into the therapy, the therapist said to Mr. Doerr: "I appreciate that your marriage came to feel awful to you and that you are pleased to be divorcing. At the same time, I find it a bit hard to believe that the marriage was as awful as you describe. Can you tell me about some close times with your wife?" Mr. Doerr, looking surprised, sat quietly and pondered. Then, he began to cry. He sat weeping for several minutes. When he recovered, he expressed shock that he was so sad. He had had no idea that he felt that way. Mr. Doerr then talked about the early years of the marriage when he and his wife were passionately in love. Over the last several years, they had drifted apart. He had believed she was responsible for that, but he was willing to consider that he had a role, too. Mr. Doerr, in the months that followed, began to mourn the end of his marriage in earnest. He sadly recalled moments of tenderness between him and his wife and reminisced mournfully about intimate family vacations.

FACILITATING THE TOLERANCE OF AMBIVALENCE THROUGH THERAPY

In the months following a separation and divorce when loss is raw, tuning oneself in to positive and negative features of a marriage simultaneously can be emotionally overwhelming. A person's defensive needs to hold tightly and single-mindedly to the negative features of the spouse, as Mr. Doerr did, blocks out awareness of sorrow at saying goodbye. However, it also impedes necessary awareness of sadness that something good has been lost. Conversely, idealizing the ex-spouse, as Ms. Adams did, obstructs awareness of realistic disappointment that also is essential to constructive mourning. Over time, the ability to tolerate ambivalence by integrating the positive and negative features of the relationship—or, put differently, the loving and hating elements—is crucial to mourning (Baum, 2006b). Wise (1980) observed that divorced women's inability to acknowledge strengths of the ex-spouse hindered the mourning process. In this context, we can suggest that the therapist's role is to facilitate the tolerance of ambivalence by helping a divorcing adult bring into awareness and bear the elements of the relationship they have defensively split off and retrospectively reframe the relationship in more complex terms.

Divorcing individuals tend to enlist therapists to buttress their defensive efforts to perceive their ex-partners in exclusively negative or positive terms, rendering recognition of their buried ambivalence challenging. Mr. Doerr, by painting his wife in vividly negative terms, successfully brought the therapist into alignment with his defensive disavowal of residual loving feelings. The therapist concluded that Mr. Doerr's wife was awful and that Mr. Doerr was lucky to escape his barren marriage. Gradually, however, by catching glimpses of Mr. Doerr's sadness and tuning in to the stilted quality of his narrative, the therapist was able to see through Mr. Doerr's defenses and recognize his sorrow right below the surface. The therapist was able to hold in his mind that Mr. Doerr must have taken the risk of asking for help because he was hurting deeply, as distinguished from asking because of his daughter, even if initially he could not put his pain into words.

Over time, if therapists can help their patients mourn, patients will rewrite their "divorce scripts" (Hetherington and Kelly, 2002). Ms. Adams was able to recognize that she chose her husband—and denied his serious problems—because of her own unresolved childhood experiences. While she remained disappointed and even somewhat angry, she also came to understand that she had colluded with him for years by denying his acting-out behaviors and thus bore at least some responsibility for the marriage dragging on as long as it had. Mr. Doerr came to recognize how hurtful his affair had been to his wife and his children. While he remained convinced that ending the marriage made sense, he recognized that his decision to flee marriage and pursue another relationship precluded efforts to improve the marriage. He realized he had become absorbed in his own needs to the exclusion of those of his family members and he determined to be more attentive to his daughter's experience of the divorce.

In helping divorced people tolerate their ambivalence, therapists must bear the powerful feelings that emerge, which places great demands on them. Some therapists, feeling that they are being rendered passive in the face of their patients' suffering, believe they have to do something to intervene (Schlesinger, 2007). Schlesinger notes that it takes a great deal of discipline "to allow a patient (or a loved one) to experience the process of grieving and mourning fully and to appreciate, and to help them appreciate, the impor-

tance of doing so" (p. 124). He suggests that therapists, by interpreting defenses against underlying sorrow, help their patients recognize new capacities to tolerate pain and thus move through a mourning process.

ADDRESSING REACTIVATED TRAUMA THROUGH THERAPY: MS. CRAWFORD

The therapy with Ms. Adams illustrates how important it is to address childhood experience in order to facilitate a constructive mourning process, especially when that experience is so intimately connected to marital difficulties.
Adults who have suffered severe trauma in childhood ~~trauma~~ tend to engage
in relationships that re-traumatize them, and, when they try to disengage
from these relationships, need help coming to terms with their early experiences.

> *Ms. Crawford was referred for a psychological evaluation after her long-term
> partner assaulted her eight-year-old son. Child Protective Services was espe-
> cially alarmed about Ms. Crawford's parenting because her partner had "ac-
> cidentally" hurt another one of her children three years earlier. In reviewing
> Ms. Crawford's history, the consulting psychologist learned that she had
> grown up with a father who sexually and physically abused her. She fled her
> childhood home at age fifteen and engaged in serial relationships with abusive
> men. She had stayed with her most recent partner for seven years, despite an
> anxious feeling that the earlier "accident" had not been accidental.*

The forces that propelled Ms. Crawford to choose—and then stay with—
abusive men tied to her inability to come to terms with her childhood experience of abuse. In such situations, the unconscious motivations for destructive
and self-destructive choices are myriad, including, from a psychoanalytic
perspective, a wish to recreate traumatic situations in order to master them, a
guilt-driven need for punishment, and, as with Ms. Crawford, an unconscious
wish to place another person (her child) in the same vulnerable position she
had been in as girl. Often, adults in Ms. Crawford's predicament are offered
treatment programs that provide lessons in understanding "power and control" and in discerning signs of trouble with a violent mate. Still, unless they
can engage in therapy to understand the powerful forces that propel them,
they are likely to continue to make tragically bad choices.

ADDRESSING THE MULTIPLE MEANINGS OF MARRIAGE/ DIVORCE TO FACILITATE MOURNING

As discussed in chapter 1, marriage and divorce have multiple meanings for
each person. In order to help a patient mourn the end of a marriage, the

therapist needs to understand the meanings of the marriage for that particular person.

In chapters 1 and 2, we met Mr. Berger, a businessman devastated by his wife's decision to divorce him. Mr. Berger struggled in the months that followed his divorce to come to terms with the end of his fifteen-year marriage. He continued to be successful at work and spend pleasant time with his children, but he still could not quite believe that his wife had chosen to leave him.

Mr. Berger's therapy focused, alternately, on different aspects of his experience. In the early years of his marriage, his wife's idealization of him had felt enlivening and sustaining. As she withdrew in the face of his burgeoning work life, he suffered a wrenching blow to his self-esteem. Mr. Berger, though highly competent professionally, came to recognize how heavily he depended on external validation of his worthiness and also how, because of his brilliance coupled with underlying insecurity, he had developed a compensatory fantasy of harboring almost magical powers to control his universe, which the end of the marriage had shattered.

Mr. Berger used the therapy as an opportunity to understand the childhood roots of his insecurities, which, to that point, he had defensively denied. It also functioned as a forum to address the lost selfobject functions and the loss of his wife herself, a once-cherished partner, as well as the family life that Mr. Berger had treasured. While he initially focused on the negative features of the marriage, he, like Mr. Doerr, was able to get in touch through therapy with his love for his wife. Being in touch with his love brought him in contact with enormous grief over losing her.

Often, it is not clear what exactly a person is mourning when she or he seeks therapy following the end of a marriage.

Ms. Epstein was referred for therapy by her attorney, who was concerned that she was being too acquiescent throughout the divorce process. Although Ms. Epstein understood she needed to get out of an abusive relationship, she felt sad, overwhelmed, and bewildered by the end of her marriage. When the therapist tried to get a sense of why she felt sad, Ms. Epstein was unable to say.

Over the course of three years in a three-sessions-per-week therapy, Ms. Epstein became able to articulate that she had recognized early on in their marriage that her husband harbored tremendous rage and was, at his worst, paranoid. She had imagined, though, that she could calm his fury if she were conciliatory and steadfast in her love. For years, his accusation that she was causing him to be angry triggered anguish that she must not be trying hard enough if he remained so disappointed in her. Ms. Epstein's sadness at the end of the marriage was rooted primarily in her need to let go of the cherished fantasy that her love could transform another person. That fantasy, rooted in traumatic childhood experiences of helplessness in relation to her parents, had served to soothe her in the face of disturbing interactions with important people in her life.

THE THERAPEUTIC RELATIONSHIP AND MOURNING

Therapy, especially more intensive therapy, by its very nature provides a rich forum for recognizing and accepting the limitations inherent in human relationships. Patients over time come to mourn the therapist's limitations (such as lapses in empathy) as well as limitations inherent in the relationship itself (for instance, the lack of physical contact, how interactions are contained within a specified time frame, and its finite nature). The emotionally laden in vivo experience of accepting limitations within a productive therapy itself facilitates a similar process in relationships out in the world. For patients struggling against mourning the end of a marriage, the experience in relation to the therapist offers powerful leverage for engaging that process more productively.

> *Ms. Epstein came to imagine that by being a "good patient" (i.e., compliant), she could transform her therapist into the more effusive man she longed for him to be. Her frustration at her limited influence over him offered her a vivid opportunity to see how she had behaved in relation to her ex-husband and to begin to clarify her fantasy that she could transform others by being amicable and conciliatory.*

> *Mr. Berger's behavior in the crucible of therapy was similarly indicative of his behavior outside it. His therapist pointed out that he was distancing himself from engagement with the therapist, which was reminiscent of how he behaved in his marriage. Mr. Berger used this observation to begin to recognize how he withdrew from relationships when he felt frustrated by their constraints and how, by withdrawing, he had contributed to the demise of his marriage.*

Therapists, by staying carefully attuned to the patient's developing transferences and listening for parallels with the marital relationship, often can make connections that facilitate a coming to terms with the end of a marriage.

> *Ms. Franz, heartbroken about the end of her marriage, spoke about her ex-husband in the most glowing of terms, glossing over his more difficult qualities. Her therapist observed that she behaved similarly with him—idealizing him as a way of avoiding acknowledging his frustrating and disappointing qualities. By pointing out the parallels between Ms. Franz's reactions to him and to her ex-husband, the therapist helped her begin to see how anxious she felt about recognizing others' imperfections. In turn, she began to consider*

that she had deep-seated needs to think of her husband as more perfect than he possibly could be.

ADDRESSING CHILD-RELATED ISSUES WITHIN AN INDIVIDUAL ADULT THERAPY

Therapists working with divorced parents in individual psychotherapy often face a dilemma: In cases of patients explicitly seeking help dealing with a child there is a clear mandate to address child-related issues, but what about those coming for help with their own emotional reactions to the divorce whose difficulties with a child emerge as the therapy progresses? Does advice-giving run contrary to good therapy practice? As time has passed, I have gradually moved to the position that therapists, if they feel they have an adequate fund of knowledge, should help their patients with their children. While it may be appropriate and useful at times to refer an adult patient to a child or adolescent therapist for a child-related consultation, doing so may not always be the best option because the adult's therapist has the clearest sense of what is contributing to that parent's problems with the child and also has established a forum in which to offer assistance.

> *Ms. Gomez sought individual psychotherapy for help with her painful emotional reactions to her divorce. Her husband had developed a severe depression that had been refractory to treatment. As he became more disabled, Ms. Gomez determined that the marriage was no longer viable. She acknowledged that she had immersed herself in work over the last few years in an effort to distance herself from her marriage. As a result, she had spent little time with her children.*

The early stages of the therapy focused on Ms. Gomez's grief about the end of her marriage and her efforts to cope with the stresses of work, the divorce, and childrearing. She felt burdened by guilt over her decision to initiate divorce yet felt liberated at the same time. As the therapy progressed, the theme of Ms. Gomez's tendency toward withdrawal came to the fore. The therapist had suggested Ms. Gomez come to multiple sessions each week, but she had resisted, citing work and financial constraints. The therapist acknowledged these but noted that she seemed to find other demands more important than therapy, as she did in the case of her family relationships.

Ms. Gomez spoke often about her sons and her concerns about the impact upon them of the divorce and their father's depression, yet she never spoke to them directly about their experience. At a certain point, the therapist observed that she appeared to avoid discussion of the tough realities in her sons' lives. He drew a parallel with her stance toward the therapy—being *partially* engaged. Ms. Gomez responded that she really did not know how to talk to her sons; her parents had never talked to her about matters of substance and the idea of initiating meaningful conversation felt foreign. In the months that followed, the therapist helped her plan discussions with the boys, using the mother/son conversations as a springboard for helping her advance her parenting in concrete ways and, when she did not follow through, helping her better understand her need to maintain distance.

Concluding Remarks

The intervention with Ms. Gomez captures many of the central issues in this book. Struggling herself with conflicted feelings about the end of her marriage, she is unable to help her children, who, in turn, are left alone with their own feelings associated with their parents' breakup. Just as her children need her help to mourn the losses in the divorce, she needs the help of the therapist who, by bearing her feelings, helps her expand her capacity to bear them. In working with divorce, therapists can be most helpful if they recognize that each family member must traverse a mourning process in face of many losses and will need steady, sensitive help in order to do so. If therapists are prepared to deal with the painful feelings that such a journey entails, they can help family members move toward creating lives less encumbered by loss.

References

Aragno, A. (2003). Transforming mourning: A new psychoanalytic perspective on the bereavement process. *Psychoanalysis and Contemporary Thought*, 28, 427–462.

Barbour, C. (1981). *Women in love: The development of feminine gender identity in the context of the heterosexual couple*. Unpublished doctoral dissertation, University of Michigan.

✳Baris, M. A., Coates, C. A., Duvall, B. B., Garrity, C. B., Johnson, E. T., and LaCrosse, E. R. (2001). *Working with high-conflict families of divorce: A guide for professionals*. Northvale, NJ: Jason Aronson, Inc.

Baum, N. (2004). Coping with "absence-presence": Noncustodial fathers' parenting behaviors. *American Journal of Orthopsychiatry*, 74 (3), 316–324.

———. (2004a). On helping divorced men to mourn their losses. *American Journal of Psychotherapy*, 58 (2), 174–185.

———. (2006). Postdivorce paternal disengagement: Failed mourning and role fusion. *Journal of Marital and Family Therapy*, 32 (2), 245–254.

———. (2006a). A Kleinian perspective on the divorce process: From the paranoid-schizoid to the depressive position, *Clinical Social Work Journal*, 34 (3), 279–291.

———. (2007). "Separation guilt" in women who initiate divorce. *Clinical Social Work*, 35, 47–55.

Betz, G., and Thorngren, J. M. (2006). Ambiguous loss and the family grieving process. *The Family Journal*, 14 (4), 359–365.

✼ Billings, J. C., Robbins, G. L., and Gordon, D. A. (2008). A high conflict divorce education program: After the storm: Surviving high conflict divorce. In Linda B. Fieldstone and Christine A. Coates (Eds.), *Innovations in interventions with high conflict families*. Madison, WI: Association of Family and Conciliation Courts.

Bowlby, J. (1963). Pathological mourning and childhood mourning. *Journal of the American Psychoanalytic Association*, 11, 500–541.

———. (1980). Processes of mourning. *The International Journal of Psychoanalysis*, 42, 317–340.

✼ Chethik, M., and Kalter, N. (1980). Developmental arrest following divorce: The role of therapist as a developmental facilitator. *Journal of the American Academy of Child Psychiatry*, 19, 281–288.

✼ Chethik, M., Plunkett, J., Colfer, M., and Lohr, R. (1984). Divorce: The parenting function and narcissistic conflict. *Journal of Preventive Psychiatry*, 2 (3 &4), 455–471.

Chethik, M., Dolin, N., Davies, D., Lohr, R., and Darrow, D. (1987). Children and divorce: The "negative" identification. In Craig A. Everett (Ed.), *The divorce process: A handbook for clinicians* (pp. 121–138). New York: Haworth.

159

Chused, J. (2012). The analyst's narcissism. *Journal of the American Psychoanalytic Association*, 60 (5), 899–916.

Coates, L. B., and Fieldstone, C. A. (2008). Introduction: Defining high conflict families. In Linda B. Fieldstone and Christine A. Coates (Eds.), *Innovations in interventions with high conflict families*. Madison, WI: Association of Family and Conciliation Courts.

Demby, S. (2009). Interparent hatred and its impact on parenting: Assessment in forensic custody evaluations. *Psychoanalytic Inquiry*, 29, 477–490.

Deutsch, R. (2011). A voice lost, A voice found: After the death of the analyst. *Psychoanalytic Inquiry*, 31 (6), 526–535.

Deutsch, R. M., Coates, C. A., and Fieldstone, L. B. (2008). Parenting coordination: An emerging role to assist high conflict families. In Linda B. Fieldstone and Christine A. Coates (Eds.), *Innovations in interventions with high conflict families*. Madison, WI: Association of Family and Conciliation Courts.

Doherty, W. J., Willoughby, B. J., and Peterson, B. (2011). Interest in marital reconciliation among divorcing parents. *Family Court Review*, 49 (2), 313–321.

Dunn, J., Davies, L., O'Connor, T., and Sturges, W. (2001). Family lives and friendships: The perspectives of children in step-, single-parent, and nonstop families. *Journal of Family Psychology*, 15, 272–287.

Ehrlich, J. (1991). *The influence of intimate heterosexual relationships during late adolescence on men's development of a masculine gender identity*. Unpublished doctoral dissertation, University of Michigan.

Ehrlich, J. (2001). Losing perspective: A danger in working with high-conflict divorces. *American Journal of Family Law*, 15 (4), 307–310

Ehrlich, J. (2011). Litigation as a defense against mourning: A perspective for attorneys and judges. *Michigan Family Law Journal*, 41 (3), 31–33.

Emery, R. E. (2012*). Renegotiating family relationships: Divorce, child custody, and mediation*. New York: The Guilford Press.

Fackrell, T. A., Hawkins, A. J., and King, N. M. (2004). How effective are court-affiliated divorcing parents education programs? A meta-analytic study. *Family Court Review*, 49 (1), 107–119.

Fidler, B. J., and Bala, N. (2010). Children resisting contact with a parent: Concepts, controversies, and conundrums. *Family Court Review*, 48 (1), 10–47.

Finley, G. E., and Schwartz, S. J. (2010). The divided world of the child: Divorce and long-term psychosocial adjustment. *Family Court Review*, 48 (3), 516–527.

Folberg, J. (1991). *Joint custody and shared parenting (Second Edition)*. New York: The Guilford Press.

Fowlkes, M. R. (1991). The morality of loss—The social construction of mourning and melancholia. *Contemporary Psychoanalysis*, 27 (3), 529–551.

Freeman. R., Abel, D., Cowper-Smith, M., and Stein, L. (2004). Reconnecting children with absent parents: A model for intervention. *Family Court Review*, 42 (3), 430-459.

Freud, S. (1917). Mourning and melancholia. *The complete psychological works of Sigmund Freud*, Volume XIV. London: The Hogarth Press.

Furman, E. (1974). *A child's parent dies: Studies in childhood bereavement*. New Haven: Yale University Press.

Gaines, R. (1997). Detachment and continuity. *Contemporary Psychoanalysis*, 33, 549–571.

Gardner, R. A. (1998). *The parental alienation syndrome (Second Edition)*. Cresskill, NJ: Creative Therapeutics.

Gorkin, M. (1984). Narcissistic personality disorder and pathological mourning. *Contemporary Psychoanalysis*, 20, 400–420.

Gunsberg, L. (2009). The developmental evolution of the family forensic evaluation. In Linda Gunsberg and Paul Hymowitz (Eds.), *A handbook of divorce and custody: Forensic, developmental, and clinical perspectives*, pp. 181–200. Hillsdale, NJ: The Analytic Press.

Hagman, G. (1995). Mourning: A review and reconsideration. *International Journal of Psychoanalysis*, 76: 909–925.

———. (1995a). Death of a selfobject: Toward a self psychology of the mourning process. *Progress in Self Psychology*, 11:189–205.

———. (1996). Bereavement and neurosis. *Journal of the American Academy of Psychoanalysis*, 23, 635–653.

———. (1996a). The role of the other in mourning. *Psychoanalytic Quarterly*, 65, 327–352.

Hetherington, E. M., and Kelly, J. (2002). *For better or for worse: Divorce reconsidered*. New York: W.W. Norton & Company.

Hodges, W. F. (1991). *Interventions for children of divorce: Custody, access, and psychotherapy (Second Edition)*. NJ: John Wiley & Sons, Inc.

Horowitz, M. (1990). A model of mourning: Change in schemas of self and other. *Journal of the American Psychoanalytic Association*, 38, 297–32.

Jacobson, G. F., and Jacobson, D. S. (1970). Impact of marital dissolution on adults and children: The significance of loss and continuity. In Jonathan Bloom-Feshbach and Sally Bloom-Feshbach (Eds.), *The psychology of separation and loss*. San Francisco: Jossey-Bass Publishers.

Johnston, J. R., and Campbell, L. E. G. (1988*). Impasses of divorce: The dynamics and resolution of family conflict*. New York: The Free Press.

Y Johnston, J. R., Roseby, V., and Kuehnle, K. (2009). *In the name of the child: A developmental approach to understanding and helping children of conflicted and violent divorce (Second Edition)*. New York: Springer Publishing Company.

Johnston, J. R., and Goldman, J. R. (2010). Outcomes of family counseling interventions with children who resist visitation: An addendum to Friedlander and Walters (2010). *Family Court Review*, 42, 622–628.

Kalter, N. (1990). *Growing up with divorce: Helping your child avoid immediate and later emotional problems*. New York: The Free Press.

Kelly, J. B., and Lamb, M. E. (2000). Using child development research to make appropriate custody and access decisions for young children. *Family and Conciliation Courts Review*, 38 (3), 297–311.

Kelly, J. B., and Emery, R. E. (2003). Children's adjustment following divorce: Risk and resilience perspectives. *Family Relations*, 52, 352–362.

Kelly, J. B., and Johnston, J. R. (2001). The alienated child: A reformulation of parental alienation syndrome. *Family Court Review*, 39, 249–266.

Klein, M. (1940). Mourning and its relation to manic-depressive states. *International Journal of Psychoanalysis*, 21, 125–153.

Kogan, I. (2007). *The struggle against mourning*. Lanham, MD: Jason Aronson.

Kohut, H. (1971). *The analysis of the self*. Chicago: University of Chicago Press.

———. (1977). *The restoration of the self*. New York: International Universities Press.

Krystal, H. (1991). Integration and self-healing in post-traumatic states: A ten year retrospective. *American Imago*, 48, 93–118.

Lande, J. (2011). An empirical analysis of collaborative practice. *Family Court Review*, 49 (2), 257–282.

Lohr, R., Chethik, M., Press, S., and Solyom, A. (1981). Impact of divorce on children: Vicissitudes and implications of the reconciliation fantasy. *Journal of Child Psychotherapy*, 7, 123–136.

Macoby, E. E., and Mnookin, R. H. (1992). *Dividing the child: Social and legal dilemmas of custody*. Cambridge, MA: Harvard University Press.

Main, M., Hesse, E., and Hesse, S. (2011). Attachment theory and research: Overview with suggested applications to child custody. *Family Court Review*, 49 (3), 426–463.

Marquardt, E. (2005). *Between two worlds: The inner lives of children of divorce*. New York: Three Rivers Press.

Mitcham-Smith, M., and Henry, W. J. (2007). High-conflict divorce solutions: Parenting coordination as a non-traditional co-parenting intervention. *Family Journal*, 15, 368–373

Mosten, F. S. (2011). The future of collaborative practice: A vision for 2030. *Family Court Review*, 49 (2), 282–300.

Neff, R., and Cooper, K. (2004). Parental conflict resolution: Six-, twelve-, and fifteen-month follow-ups of a high-conflict program. *Family Court Review*, 42 (1), 99–114.

Ogden, T. (2002). A new reading on the origins of object-relations theory. *International Journal of Psychoanalysis*, 83, 767–782.

Pedro-Carroll, J. (2010). *Putting children first: Proven parenting strategies for helping children thrive through divorce.* New York: The Penguin Group.

Pedro-Carroll, J., Nakhnikian, E., and Montes, G. (2001). Assisting children through transition: Helping parents protect their children from the toxic effects of ongoing conflict in the aftermath of divorce. *Family Court Review,* 39, 377–392.

Person, E. S. (1986). Male sexuality and power. *Psychoanalytic Inquiry,* 6:3–25.

———. (1988). *Dreams of love and fateful encounters: The power of romantic passion.* New York: W.W. Norton & Company.

Parens, H. (2001). An obstacle to the child's coping with object loss. In Salman Akhtar (Ed.), *Three faces of mourning: Melancholia, manic defense and moving on,* pp. 157–183. New York: Jason Aronson.

Price, J. A. (1996). *Power and compassion: Working with difficult adolescents and abused parents.* New York: The Guilford Press.

Pruett, M. K., Ebling, R., and Insabella, G. (2004). Critical aspects of parenting plans for young children. *Family Court Review,* 42 (1), 39–59.

Rice, J. K., and Rice, D. G. (1986). *Living through divorce: A developmental approach to divorce therapy.* New York: The Guilford Press.

Rye, M., Folck, C., Heim, T., Olszewski, B., and Traina, E. (2004). Forgiveness of an ex-spouse: How does it relate to mental health following a divorce. *Journal of Divorce and Remarriage,* 41 (3/4), 31–51.

Schafer, R. (1983). *The analytic attitude.* London: Hogarth Press, Ltd.

Schlesinger, H. (2007). Technical problems in analyzing the mourning patient. In Salman Akhtar (Ed.), *Three faces of mourning: Melancholia, manic defense, and moving on,* pp. 115–139. New York: Jason Aronson.

Settlage, C. (2007). Defenses evoked by early childhood loss: Their impact on life-span development. In Salman Akhtar (Ed.), *Three faces of mourning: Melancholia, manic defense and moving on,* pp. 47–93. New York: Jason Aronson.

Shane, E., and Shane, M. (1990). Object loss and selfobject loss: A consideration of self psychology's contribution to understanding mourning and the failure to mourn. *Annual of Psychoanalysis,* 18, 115–131.

Singer, J. B. (2009). Dispute resolution and the postdivorce family: Implications of a paradigm shift. *Family Court Review,* 47 (3), 363–370.

Slochower, J. (1993). Mourning and the holding function of shiva. *Contemporary Psychoanalysis,* 29, 352–367.

Socarides, D., and Stolorow, R. (1984). Affects and selfobjects. *Annual of Psychoanalysis,* 12, 105–119.

Steiner, J. (2005). The conflict between mourning and melancholia. *Psychoanalytic Quarterly,* 74, 83–104.

Strohschein, L. (2007). Challenging the presumption of diminished capacity to parent: Does divorce really change parenting practices? *Family Relations,* 56, 358–368.

Sullivan, M. J., Ward, P. A., and Deutsch, R. M. (2010). Overcoming barriers family camp: A program for high-conflict divorced families where a child is resisting contact with a parent. *Family Court Review,* 48 (1), 116–135.

Tessman, L. H. (1996). *Helping children cope with parting parents.* Northvale, NJ: Jason Aronson, Inc.

Vaillant, G. (1977). *Adaptation to life: How the best and brightest came of age.* Boston: Little, Brown and Company.

Wallerstein, J. S. (1990). Transference and countertransference in clinical interventions with divorcing families. *American Journal of Orthopsychiatry,* 60 (3), 337–345.

Wallerstein, J. S., and Kelly, J. B. (1980). *Surviving the breakup.* New York: Basic Books.

Wallerstein, J. S., and Blakeslee, S. (1989). *Second chances: Men, women and children a decade after divorce.* New York: Tichnor and Fields.

Wallerstein, J. S., Lewis, J. M., and Blakeslee, S. (2000). *The unexpected legacy of divorce: The 25 year landmark study.* New York: Hyperion.

Warshak, R. A. (1992). *The custody revolution: The father factor and the motherhood mystique.* New York: Poseidon Press.

————. (2010). Family bridges: Using insights from social science to reconnect parents and alienated children. *Family Court Review*, 48 (1), 48–80.

Waters, E., and McIntosh, J. (2011). Are we asking the right questions about attachment? *Family Court Review*, 49 (3), 474–482.

Wilson, M. (2004). The analyst's desire and narcissistic resistances. *Journal of the American Psychoanalytic Association*, 51 (1), 71–99.

Wise, M. (1980). The aftermath of divorce. *American Journal of Psychoanalysis*, 40, 149–158.

Index

absent parents: identification with, 39–40,
   136; mourning for, 98–100; reaching
   out to, 97–98
adolescents, 80; age-appropriate separation
   and, 67; aggression of, 39; anger of,
   66–67; communication with parents,
   139; coordinating care for, 141–142;
   co-parenting of, 65–66;
   countertransference and, 140–141; in
   danger, 66–67; divorcing parents and,
   65–67; empathy of, 67; guilt of, 138; in
   high-conflict divorce, 68–69; parenting
   challenges for, 63–64; sexual
   relationships of, 66; therapy for,
   137–142, 143–146
adult therapy, 149; child-related issues in,
   157–158; mourning in, 149–152, 156;
   multiple meanings of marriage and
   divorce in, 154–156; reactivated trauma
   in, 154; tolerance of ambivalence in,
   152–154
"After the Storm" (community-based
   program), 126
aggression, 25; of adolescents, 39; of
   children, 39, 41; hypochondriasis and,
   31
agreements, pre-divorce, 36–37
alienation, parental, 129–131
ambiguity, 121–123
ambiguous loss, 73–74
ambivalence, tolerance of, 152–154

anger, 52, 105; of adolescents, 66–67; of
   children, 39
Aragno, A., 13
arguments, 37, 56
attachments, 8; narcissistic, 24, 25;
   primary, 136
autonomy, 63
Axis II diagnoses, 27

Baris, M. A., 107, 121
Baum, Nehami, 17, 19, 44, 98
behavior modification programs, 106
"between-two-worlds" experience, 35, 46;
   addressing, 103–104; coordination and,
   91; transitions and, 103, 104
Billings, J. C., 126
Blakeslee, S., 39, 89
Bowlby, J., 13, 73

Campbell, L. E. G., ix; on high-conflict
   divorce, 27, 59, 143; on immature and
   psychotic defenses, 30; on narcissistic
   disturbance, 121; on non-acrimonious
   interactions, 22; on parenting
   arrangements, 92; on short-term
   interventions, 143; on social
   dislocation, 7; on tribal warfare, 31
Chethik, M., 121, 136
childhood experiences: marriage and, 3–4,
   6; reactivated trauma and, 154

About the Author

Joshua Ehrlich, PhD, is a clinical psychologist and psychoanalyst who works with children, adolescents and adults in his practice in Ann Arbor, MI. He is an adjunct clinical instructor in the Department of Psychiatry at the University of Michigan and Faculty at the Michigan Psychoanalytic Institute. He graduated from Wesleyan University with a degree in English, then received his doctorate in clinical psychology at the University of Michigan. He completed his psychoanalytic training at the Michigan Psychoanalytic Institute. In the last twenty five years, he has worked with hundreds of divorcing families as a custody evaluator, parenting coordinator, mediator and therapist.

CPSIA information can be obtained at www.ICGtesting.com
Printed in the USA
BVOW05*2338090514

352886BV00002BA/4/P